ALIYA

Home. Hope. Reality.

Ariella Bernstein
Avi Losice

Loeb Publishing, Lawrence, New York

Printed in the United States

Library of Congress Control Number: 2020924013

Bernstein, Ariella
Losice, Abraham
Aliya: Home. Hope. Reality. /
by Ariella Bernstein, Abraham (Avi) Losice p. cm.
Includes bibliographical references and index. ISBN 978-1-7362018-1-7
First edition

Dedicated to our parents
Rivka and Moshe Losice, Of Blessed Memory
and
Drs. Deena and Josh Bernstein

"A cord of three strands is not quickly broken"

(Ecclesiastes, Chapter 4, Verse 12)

For our children and grandchildren we left behind
Leah, Elishah, Rafi, Naftali, Benjy, Gavriel, and Nava

"וׁשבו בנים לגבולם"

Children shall return to these borders

(Jeremiah, Chapter 31, Verse 16)

And for the brave young olim we have come to know so well
Jacob, Yitzie, Michal, Avital, Tali, Doron, Eliana, and Jacques

ALIYA

Home. Hope. Reality.

Ariella Bernstein
Avi Losice

Contents

Introduction

On August 18, 2009, we boarded an El Al flight and made aliya to Israel. Ariella was 41; the children were 13 and 8. Avi joined the flight, helped the family get adjusted, but continued to work in the United States. His aliya was completed five and a half years later.

No one forgets their aliya date, and not just because we fill out the same date over and over on nearly every government-related document. We remember our aliya day for the emotions it evokes. The blessings parents give their children right before they step into airport security's point of no return. The parents who could not bear to watch you leave, so they dropped you off at the curb. The parents who helped you push the overstuffed duffle bags through check-in while holding back tears. The siblings who confidently whisper in your ear, "We will join you soon," when there is very little chance of that happening. The grandparents who are grateful they lived to see the birth of their grandchildren yet now face an ocean-size geographic separation.

By all accounts, we were adults when we made aliya; we understood that our formerly successful careers could take a hit, we grasped the soberness of our decision, and we subconsciously (or maybe consciously) knew that we were entering a culture that was difficult to navigate—and not just because of the language. We were convinced we were wise enough and mature enough to appreciate that challenges lie ahead, and we had some degree of certainty that we could overcome them. We got some of it right and some of it wrong, but this book isn't about our story.

It's about olim (Israeli immigrants) whose suitcases are jam-packed with hopes and dreams, enthusiasm and eagerness, a healthy dose of chutzpah and virtually no fear, and it is a guide for parents whose idealistic children slipped out of their grasp, leaving them to cope with mixed feelings of pride and apprehension. Parents who, for the first time in their lives, feel they are ill-equipped to ease their children's transition to adulthood or their own parenthood, or who look into the future and see a world of missed opportunities with their grandchildren. In 2019, aliya rates were higher than usual, with more than 33,000 immigrants to Israel,[1] a little more than 30% of them (10,540) ages 15-35.[2] This book is for them, for those who dream of following in their footsteps, and for parents and grandparents who are, or will be, left behind to face a future with their loved ones far away.

It is often difficult to write a guide like this one when targeting different audiences—olim, parents, and grandparents. Each group can have diametrically opposed views and emotions stemming from the same event—making aliya. But we have seen, experienced, and been involved with all sides of the parent-oleh-grandparent relationship. And because we are American and Israeli, we have a deep appreciation for what olim undergo, coupled with heartfelt empathy for parents who feel unmoored or disconnected from their children's experiences.

Most people won't remember what others said, and most won't remember what they've read. But they will remember how you made them feel, and that is the entire raison d'être of this book: to move people and inject the aliya process with a dose of emotion so that we all handle it—and our relationships—better.

Today, there are many resources for olim and their parents, and we make no attempt to replace them. There are a plethora of organizations and social media groups available like never before. Nefesh B'Nefesh is undeniably a vast and phenomenal source of information, with staff that are more than willing to help North American olim and parents with questions. There are Facebook groups dedicated to assisting olim from any corner of the world. Nonprofits abound to help olim from anywhere of any age group.

Online resources are plenty, but our encounters with olim who left their families at the departure gate led us to write this book. We attempt to reconcile the experiences of olim and their new philosophy on life with their families' thirst for rational explanations that drive their choices, decisions that can be at odds with advice from family and friends.

In recent years, some 30,000 immigrants of all ages have arrived in Israel annually, the majority from former Soviet bloc countries. In fact, two out of three immigrants to Israel are from Russia or the Ukraine,[3] and only about 10% come from North America. According to 2020 research by Israel's leading demographer Sergio DellaPergola, ideology often explains the decision in principle to move to Israel but, more often than not, unemployment explains the timing of the move for those from Russia, Argentina, and Mexico. When it comes to the United States, "the roots of the Jewish working population are so deep, so successful, and so extensive," DellaPergola noted, "that you don't just give that up to move to a smaller country with a much smaller market and with fewer opportunities for mobility."[4]

Olim from North America are often prepared to leave behind an easier existence because they truly believe that they belong in Israel. Those who immigrate from Russia, Ukraine, England, France, and South and Central America often come to Israel because they see their Jewish communities as lacking in one way or another. They come to the Jewish homeland to live in a country that is rich in Jewish culture and steeped in tradition, a place where their Jewish future is more developed, and to build a home where Jewish identity is ingrained.

Regardless of the reasons olim immigrate, every oleh's experience is unique, as is every parent's or grandparent's relationship with their children or grandchildren. This book should not be interpreted as hard-and-fast solutions to the stresses that come with aliya. It is purely a "guide to the perplexed" for olim who are dumbfounded by their family's incessant need to seemingly wrap their arms around a life they will never understand and for parents who are stymied by how best to steer their children through a cultural landmine that is thousands of miles away.

As is our practice in our own home, we try to steer clear of encouraging or discouraging aliya, for these decisions are highly personal. We'll go one step further. The decision to make aliya is not only personal, but emotional, and attempts by olim of any age to explain their reasoning or rationalize it to their families is often met by equally reasonable counterarguments against making aliya.

Our only goal in this book is to provide logistical, rational, and emotional guidance for olim and their families once a decision is made.

An invincible mindset is an asset in the rough and tumble of Israeli life, and it is often accompanied by an oleh's constant refrain, "Look, Mom, you just don't understand Israel." We have been on the receiving end of this very refrain from our own children.

To the olim out there, we concede that your parents might not understand Israel, but know that they understand *you*. Any suggestions they make often come from their love and concern for you. Olim who shut their parents or family members out by errors of commission or omission do themselves and their parents an injustice.

To the parents who reside in another time zone, or in communities you are convinced were more than adequate for your children, we concede that your children might not have fully considered the ramifications of making aliya, but know that you will always understand your child better than anyone on the planet. This stage of parenting will have you traveling down an uncharted road in a foreign land with language and cultural challenges for you, yet you still have a role in your children's transformational journey even when you are accused of zero comprehension.

This book is arranged by topic. In each case, we explore what olim might be going through; how family members might view the same event or experience; where and when misunderstandings can arise; and what can be done to alleviate complications, remove obstacles, and create an atmosphere that is simultaneously helpful to olim and their families left behind. We also include the results of our survey, with responses from nearly 300 olim and their parents, which buttressed the conclusions we drew. Key terms are defined in the margins and in the Glossary of Terms at the end of this book. This book is not intended to be comprehensive, and there are likely other points to be made that we have failed to address. Any errors are our own.

On August 19, 2009, after an 11-hour emotionally grueling flight, we landed in Israel. Overnight, the staff of Nefesh B'Nefesh processed our paperwork on the plane, and by the time we arrived, we were already Israeli citizens. Nefesh B'Nefesh so aptly created the hashtag **#LivingTheDream**, and it accurately reflects what you feel in that poignant moment.

In the years since, we have been privileged to meet so many olim who relived that same poignant moment when their hopes and dreams finally came to fruition and they arrived home. And we witnessed the adjustment period that followed, from "#LivingTheDream" to living the reality. We hope that this book helps olim, and the families they leave behind, navigate that emotional journey together, so that we all handle aliya—and our relationships—better.

Famous Israeli Last Words:

יהיה בסדר
"It will be ok."

Sometimes it is.
Sometimes it isn't.

1

How About
College
First?

"An investment in knowledge always pays the best interest."

—Benjamin Franklin, The Way to Wealth [1]

On average, approximately 30,000 olim of all ages immigrate to Israel annually. Two out of three are from Russia or the Ukraine and about 10% are from North America, leaving small percentages from Europe or South America.[2]

More than 33,000 immigrated to Israel in 2019,[3] and of them, 10,540 were ages 15-35.[4] Some might have visited Israel with their parents; others might have toured Israel on a Birthright program or even spent a gap year in Israel. And, of course, there are olim who might never have visited at all. Olim who come from Russia or the Ukraine likely have their sights set on Israel because their Jewish communities "at home" are lacking (at best) or because they face some level of anti-Semitism (at worst). Either way, all olim have a few basic things in common. They feel that Israel is their home, it is where they belong, and they come filled with hope for their future. Nothing beats youth and exuberance.

Some olim are quite young when they make the decision to move to Israel without their families, although they need to be at least 18 to apply for Israeli citizenship without parental permission. Most adolescents around the world begin to take their first steps toward independence, but moving to Israel on their own is an independent step of a much higher magnitude.

Olim ages 18-20 are occasionally bitten by the Zionism bug during summer trips or a gap year program. Gap year programs in Israel generally cover a wide variety of disciplines. More religious programs cover standard subjects like Torah or Talmudic study, Jewish history, Jewish philosophy, and perhaps studies in Zionism. Less religious programs cover Jewish history, Zionism concepts, Jewish social justice, and cultural texts. If the gap year program sits within an Israeli university setting, studies might focus on academic and/ or university level subjects. There is, however, a common denominator among nearly all gap year programs: travel days throughout Israel to experience life.[5]

Research shows that structured gap year programs serve to develop individuals into more focused students with a better sense of purpose and engagement in the world.[6] Not every Jewish high school student enrolls in an Israeli gap year program, but those who do likely find the experience "freeing," particularly in situations where the gap year student never really spent significant periods away from parents. Overall, it is probably not all that different from any incoming freshman who leaves home for a college dorm room.[7]

Gap year students, and those who have vacationed in Israel during the summer, travel the length and breadth of the country, meeting "real" Israelis, including soldiers of the same age who are drafted into mandatory army service. Undeniably, these encounters give an impression of what life is like in an exotic country, and students might return home feeling so inspired that they are convinced this life is for them.

Aliya from Russia, the Ukraine, parts of Europe, and South America is likely triggered by a desire for a richer Jewish identity, something that young olim from these regions feel they lack in their Diaspora Jewish communities. They might have been planning their aliya for some time, seen others make the journey before them, and involved their parents in their decisions at a much earlier stage.

But young adults who have been on an Israeli gap year program might casually mention their love of Israel and their desire for aliya during their gap year communications with their parents. Some might wait until they return home to drop this life-altering news. Others who have been accepted to university might be prepared to forgo their enrollment, and if there are "undecideds" among gap year students, they might see aliya as an appealing solution.

A haphazardly planned or spontaneous aliya by an

18- or 19-year-old student during or immediately after a gap year program is probably not wise. But it is possible. In this situation, it is unlikely that discussions about aliya were fully aired with parents prior to the gap year, and in-person communications are quite limited during a gap year program. Under all circumstances, we believe that making aliya during a gap year is ill-advised. If gap year students attempt to make aliya from Israel during their gap year, they will likely need parental assistance in gathering all of the appropriate forms, and it is here that parents can have some leverage. Parents will most likely (and rightfully) instruct their children to return home to their "real life." Gap year programs are far from authentic Israeli living; parents know this and defer any discussion on aliya until the gap year is over.

Young adults from smaller Jewish communities around the world, or at least ones they view as lacking a Jewish identity or cultural connection, will often contend that their future is in the Jewish state. On some level, their aliya is a rational decision rooted in the notion that Israel is a place where they find their commonality with other Jews, where they can find a Jewish spouse and raise children with a bare minimum of Jewish association or identity. For these young adults, Israel is the *only* place for them. Parents and young olim who don't share the same level of commitment to Jewish identity might find themselves at odds when it comes to aliya.

Regardless of an oleh's country of origin, parents might fall anywhere on the aliya spectrum between largely supportive conceptually and openly hostile. No matter where they are on the scale, parents of olim of any age often focus their discussions on "why," seeking rational, logical, and thoughtful explanations for the move to Israel. Parents will hammer home that gap year programs do not represent what life will be like in Israel, a truthful statement if there ever was one. And when all this reasonableness fails and the inspired, spirited child insists on going anyway, parents can play the "finish college first and then we will talk" card. Even in cases where parents understand the limitedness of their Jewish community, they can have a hard time accepting aliya. One way or another, a parent's response to aliya can range from outright hostility to mildly supportive. We find that parents ultimately resign themselves to the concept of aliya, and those who are happy about their child's aliya often find their happiness tempered by sadness at the geographic distance.

Overall, the "college card" is not a bad hand to play. Chances are that the post-gap year student applied and has been accepted to university, tuition perhaps was partially paid, dorm rooms were reserved, and plans were made, all of which fully involved the gap year student during the last few years of high school. If you spend years planning your academic higher education, it is reasonable to take the position that you have already charted a course to college, time and perhaps money were invested, and you should see the decision through to the end.

We asked olim and their parents about the college debate—whether it arose during aliya discussions and why. Of the nearly 300 olim and parents, of all ages, who answered our survey, three quarters (75%) of olim did not have a university degree before they made aliya. But, was there a discussion between olim and parents about completing a degree before aliya? On this, there seems to be a fair amount of disagreement, as noted in Figure 1.

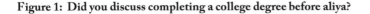

Figure 1: Did you discuss completing a college degree before aliya?

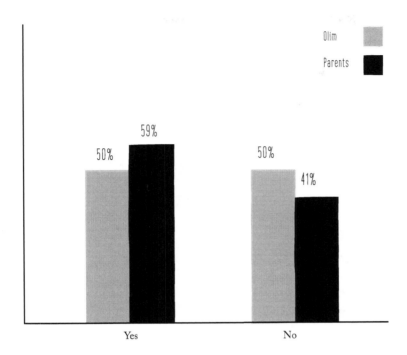

Yes   No

Olim are split 50-50 as to whether the subject of a degree pre-aliya was discussed, but when comparing parents vs. olim, 9% more of the parents said they discussed a degree before their child made aliya.

We also asked olim and parents why the topic of a university degree arose. A total of 258 respondents answered. Figure 2 breaks down their responses numerically.

Even though 75 respondents indicated that the issue did not come up at all, 183 respondents in nearly all cases selected more than one answer, indicating that the subject, in one way or another, arose. The multiplicity of answers from most respondents suggests that during these discussions, the issue came up from a number of angles.

Figure 2: A college degree prior to aliya was raised for the following reasons:

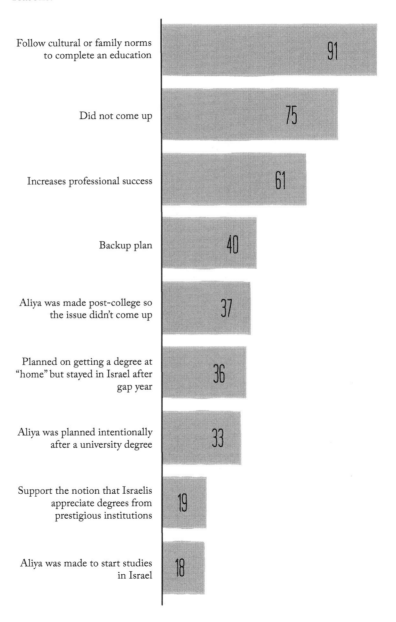

Anecdotally, we heard from a number of olim that parents expressed concern that university was not part of post-aliya plans. As a result, we asked to what extent was there concern that university was not part of an oleh's plans. The results are in Figure 3.

Figure 3: I/Parents were concerned that attending college/university was not part of a post-aliya plan

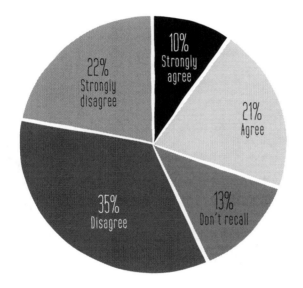

The majority (57%) strongly disagree/disagree that there were any concerns about university post-aliya, compared to 31% who agreed that this was an issue.

The Dialogue

When the topic of aliya is raised by an 18- to 20-year-old, the debate that ensues with parents can go something like this:

Oleh   Parents

"A university education gives you a profession for life, so why not complete it and then move?"

"I spoke to people my age in Israel. College is so much cheaper in Israel. You'd be saving money!"

"You never mentioned any of this during high school. All of this is new, so why not complete what you planned?"

"You think that my passion for Israel will go away just because you force me to finish college here? It won't, and you are just trying to delay the inevitable."

"Gap year experiences, on our dime, are not real life, so let's get back to reality and finish college."

"I will be able to support myself. If I go into the army, I get extra pay, and there are all sorts of benefits for olim, so I won't need your help."

"You will be better prepared for life if you finish college here."

"What I do in the army is more important for job placement than anything else."

These scenarios have the best of intentions. When confronted with their child's newly found idealism that might not have been mentioned until then, parents resort to very logical arguments. And, those arguments are based largely on parents' own experiences. University really is the beginning of and a solid foundation for professional life. An all-expenses-paid gap year romanticizes life abroad. The journey to finding the right college started long ago and might have been a done deal before the gap year began. And again, even where parents acknowledge the limitations of their Jewish community, somehow acceptance of aliya remains difficult, and parents might offer a variety of incentives to get their children to stay put. It might even be that parents play the "finish college first" card because they often don't understand how colleges or careers work in Israel.

The responses of olim to their parents' arguments are often based on youthful inexperience, although they genuinely feel that they are on the receiving end of a bait and switch. They sincerely believe a quid pro quo is in the offing, that a college degree is a condition precedent to parental consent to aliya or that some other parental promise will give them reserved support in the future. Most young olim don't believe that they will actually secure their parents' blessing in three or four years, no matter what parents offer as an incentive to postpone aliya.

Both sides are misguided when it comes to the validity of pre-aliya college. With all due respect to the idealistic young adults, counterarguments to their parents' well-reasoned positions miss the point altogether. The same goes for the parents. Your arguments might be logically based on your life experiences, but they are not fully applicable in Israel.

⍉ Reality Check

The reality is that encouraging a college degree before aliya might suit parents' motivation to keep children under their wing or buy time in the hopes that children change their minds. But there is little nexus between a successful college experience and a successful *klita,* absorption in Israel society, for these reasons:

Klita
*Absorption
into Israeli
society.*

- **Israeli university eases absorption:** *Klita* into Israeli society and preparation for a career in Israel are far smoother if olim attend an Israeli college or university,[8] if for nothing else than language capability and shared experiences with other Israelis their own age who start college in their mid-20s.

- **There is little prestige in the age-old adage "my son/daughter the doctor":** The traditional Jewish social fabric of "my son/daughter the doctor" or "my son/daughter the lawyer" simply doesn't apply in Israel. To be frank, an entrepreneur or a freelancer can make more money than a doctor who spends 10 years or more in school. Lawyers in Israel are a dime a dozen, and those who came with law degrees in hand often reinvent themselves. A "former" lawyer might decide to establish a startup. A doctor who might have been a frequent flier for his medical practice gives it up to make peanut butter—a true story![9]

- **The IDF:** Mandatory draft is a significant and societally honored detour from college in Israel. Drafted olim are two to three years away from walking through the hallowed halls of a university. The army experience is so overwhelming that, for this reason alone, college is far from their minds (see Chapter 7, "IDF/National Service").

■ **Debt-laden costs of Diaspora higher education:** Debt is a significant part of most American students' post-college life. If your child will have student loan payments, it is highly improbable to expect to be able to make those payments on an Israeli salary.

■ **International degrees carry less weight:** Degrees from overseas institutions, even from the best in the world, are not nearly as valued in Israel. Simply put, a degree from an Ivy League college or its equivalent the world over has less impact than you think on an oleh's ability to find gainful employment. Parents playing the college card might very well lack understanding of Israel's higher education system or the employment market.

■ **It is common to switch careers in today's modern world:** Dovetailing from the point above, young people today all over the world switch jobs every two to three years. It is a function of modern-day life. Young adults today make unconventional decisions, and an oleh's career choice does not fit the mold of what a respectable education or career looks like to a parent outside of Israel. A financially "successful" career outside of Israel often does not translate *in* Israel, which is the reason many olim reinvent themselves.

☐ Reframing the College Debate

Both sides in this debate have good intentions, yet it can stress the relationship between parents and children. We recommend that potential olim and their parents keep in mind the following:

Olim: Appreciate, respect, and understand where your parents are coming from, even if you plan on ignoring their advice. Most parents grew up on the concept that college really is the foundation for a career; that is how your parents experienced it, and they want the same for you, even if you believe that they are "stalling for time." However, Israel's relatively low tuition costs and the financial support you receive from the government will not alleviate the challenges you will have in an Israeli college. College in Israel will be hard if nothing else because your language skills will take time to develop to university acceptable levels, even if you serve in the IDF or National Service.

Parents: Recognize that the college degree, as you know it, has little impact on your children's success in Israel. So many other factors are part and parcel of their absorption, most of which are out of your control. Leveraging the college degree hoping your children's aliya infatuation will fade probably won't serve your children well if they decide to make aliya anyway. The best you can do is keep the lines of communication open, understand that many young people today change careers a few times, and what you see as a successful education or career does not necessarily translate in Israel. If you accept these premises, the lines of communication remain open so that when your children start applying to college in Israel or start considering a career path, they can turn to you as a sounding board when they have to make complex decisions (see Chapter 8, "University" for a greater description of higher education in Israel).

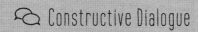

Constructive Dialogue

Olim
"I will be going to college."

Parents
"Let us know when you are ready. Perhaps we can help guide you."

2

Can You At Least Explain Why?

"I'm sure you have some cosmic rationale."

—Billy Joel, "Pressure" [1]

For the past decade, our Shabbat table has been graced by hundreds of guests. Most visited for short periods with no intention of aliya. We have hosted university level or gap year students, IDF lone soldiers, post-service lone soldiers, the educated with some career experience, tourists, and so on. More often than we can remember, our guests simply came to us via a WhatsApp message or a fourth-degree connection to us. Whenever we encounter a tourist, a student, or even businesspeople coming to Israel, we regularly invite them to our home for Shabbat.

Young adults and families contemplating aliya have been frequent guests in our home. Some are our children's friends; others are the children of our friends or distant relatives. No matter who they are or how close they are to us, we have a hard and fast rule. We neither encourage nor discourage aliya, because it is a highly personal decision. Some of our guests might say that we lean toward discouraging aliya or, at the bare minimum, we are abundantly clear about the challenges young olim will face.

But when we do hear that one of our guests has decided to make aliya, whether that decision is final or remains ambiguous, we ask them why. What's the rationale, the passionate story, the motivation behind the desire to move to Israel?

We will cut to the chase. There is no right answer, although there are obviously wrong ones. It is generally a bad idea to move to Israel if you are running away from a personal problem in your home country. Chances are that problems will follow you here. It is an equally bad idea to move to Israel because you and your parents don't see eye to eye or because there is tension between you and your parents on the subject of Jewish identity. Very few young olim openly admit to tension with their parents as their motivation for making aliya, but it is detectable if you listen closely.

We listen carefully to what lies behind olim's desire to move to Israel. Again, there is no correct answer, but the younger the olim, the more likely that their reasoning will include some sort of "high" associated with experiences here. It is important to come down from that high, look at the issue from all angles, and then decide.

Figure 1: What were the reasons given for aliya?

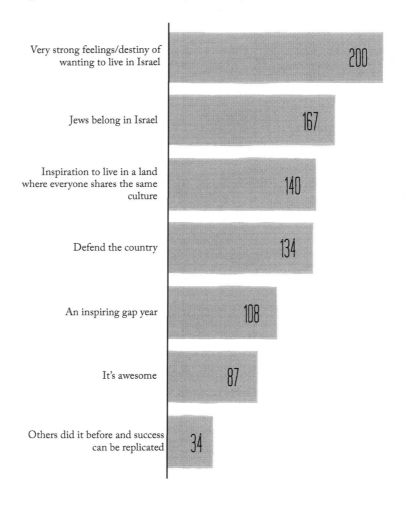

We surveyed olim and parents to better understand the "why" behind aliya. The question allowed respondents to select multiple answers. A total of 263 responses were received, and each response averaged more than three and a half selections per respondent. Figure 1 reflects the numeric breakdown.

A majority of respondents led with destiny-related feelings or belonging, such as a strong desire to live in Israel, the homeland of the Jewish people where there is cultural "Jewishness." Only 10 responses indicated that the olim came to defend the country alone, something we applaud because, in our view, moving to Israel just to join the IDF might not be best idea. We also isolated the "it's awesome" response and found that no one indicated that this was their sole reason for making aliya—and we applaud it, since we believe that this reason alone fails to account for the difficulties of aliya. Indeed, in a separate question, nearly 100% of all respondents strongly agreed/agreed with the statement that there are challenges associated with aliya. Among some of the free-text comments submitted, a handful (8) indicated that they moved to Israel to escape anti-Semitism, and a few (3) added that they came to Israel to marry within the faith.

As indicated above, we asked olim and parents to what extent they agreed with the statement that there are challenges associated with making aliya. Nearly 100% of respondents agreed/strongly agreed, and we therefore were interested in understanding what concerns were raised about aliya. A total of 266 people responded to this multiple-choice question. Figure 2 reflects those responses.

Figure 2: Concerns raised about aliya

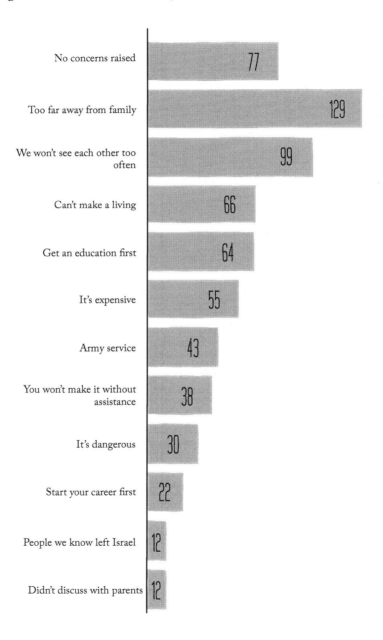

Setting aside those who said there were no concerns expressed at all, the average respondent mentioned three different concerns.

We also asked olim what they wish they had known before they made aliya. Some of the answers included "be prepared for anything and everything"; "it's important to know and be confident in your reasons because it definitely isn't easy"; "come as young as you can"; "do it when you are really ready, do research, and prepare"; "find a support network, don't be afraid to ask for help"; "learn the language"; "a trip makes things look fun and better, but once you become a citizen, that's when the **** hits the fan"; "it's a big transition, so come with an open mind"; "there are so many things that you only figure out after moving, there is never enough information, everyone makes mistakes, it's frustrating but you learn as you go"; and "don't compare your country of origin to Israel." All these concepts are words of wisdom from olim whose excitement took priority when they made aliya and, in hindsight, wished they'd kept all of the above in mind. We would only add one more concept. If you manage your expectations, you will be less frustrated.

Most olim, particularly younger ones, will not be consciously aware of any of these issues at the time they make the decision to move. If you raise these issues with them, they are likely to say, "Yes, yes, I know." But they don't.

As indicated earlier, our data showed that nearly 100% of respondents conceded that there are challenges associated with aliya, yet when we asked whether those challenges were discussed between parents and olim, the data shows a gap between the views of parents and olim, as noted in Figure 3.

Figure 3: The challenges associated with aliya were discussed between parents and olim

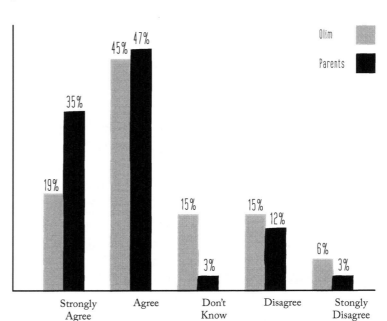

Figure 3 shows that, at some level, olim and their parents agree that they discussed the challenges, but parents are far more certain than olim (they strongly agree more, by 16%) that they discussed the challenges. Perhaps parents brought up challenges but olim did not want to discuss them.

The time eventually comes when olim sit down with their parents to break the news, keeping none of the above in mind because it is nary a thought in their head. As we indicated in Chapter 1, under all circumstances, we would discourage any decision to make aliya during a gap year. Post-gap year students who are determined to make aliya will drop a series of hints about it or might want to have an official "sit down" with their parents.

💬 The Dialogue

Whether it comes up haphazardly or in a structured manner, the debate between olim and their parents about aliya is generally rife with arguments in favor of aliya and equally counterargued by parents. The conversation can go something like this:

Oleh   Parents

"I am a Jew and I belong here."

"You can be a Jew here too."

"I want to live in a place where Jewish identity is clear, where my culture and holidays are the majority—not the minority."

"We live in a Jewish community that honors Jewish culture, tradition, and holidays. Why can't you stay here and be Jewish?"

"I want to defend the country."

"I read somewhere that lone soldiers have a really hard time adjusting."

"I want to be part of making history in a Jewish country."

"That's very admirable, but we can just as well support those who are making history."

"I can totally do this. I will do my service, I will get assistance from *Misrad HaKlita,* and I will be fine."

"Do you know how many people we know who made aliya, even older than you, and who came back because they just couldn't make it?"

"You raised me to love and support Israel."

"Yes, but I didn't mean that you should move there."

"I really thought this through; here is my plan, and I can make it."

"The best-laid plans. Have you ever noticed how many people in Israel rely on support from people outside of Israel?"

Of course, these are not the only options, and we have heard some very shallow reasons for aliya. Our all-time favorite is, "Israel is awesome," as mentioned in the survey question earlier. In most cases, the discussions surrounding aliya continue for weeks or months, covering the same ground over and over. Young olim find different ways of expressing their passion for Israel while parents come back with more inquiries, with a phrase that might start with, "Have you thought about [fill in the blank]?" Eventually, someone breaks. And it doesn't matter if aliya is motivated by a desire to be part of a larger Jewish community that is missing in the Diaspora or whether it is motivated by a deeply held spirit of Zionism that makes them want to destabilize their otherwise stable future.

Both sides come to these discussions backed by healthy doses of passion for their own positions. There is nothing like the idealism of youth. Young adults have optimism in spades; it is the engine that drives them and, to be fair, we raise them that way. By the time we become parents, we are more closely aligned to the Mark Twain saying, "As I slowly grow wise I briskly grow cautious." We evaluate more carefully because we have more responsibility, and we are often less likely to take risks. The statistics show that even born Israelis leave the country, demonstrating that life in Israel is far from utopia (see Chapter 13, "And If All Else Fails").

⊘ Reality Check

The reality is that aliya is an emotional choice, not a rational one. When parents' life-long experiences backed by logic crash headfirst into their children's passion, it can be a painful and perhaps unwinnable battle.

In the past decade (2009-2019), Israel absorbed about 250,000 immigrants, with 2019 alone representing the largest annual figure in a decade, marking 33,000 olim. Russian olim lead the way with some 66,800 people who emigrated over the past 10 years, followed by the Ukraine (45,670), France (38,000), the United States (32,000), and Ethiopia (10,500).[2]

Russian, Ukrainian, French, and Ethiopian immigration is generally fueled by a less-than-ideal environment for Jews in those countries, circumstances that are less applicable to Jews who live in the United States, Canada, Australia, and some parts of Western Europe. Using the statistics from the past decade, the average annual aliya from America is about 3,200 per year; if you include Canada, it is likely that the average annual North American aliya rate is about 3,500.[3]

Every year, the Israeli government reports on the number of Israelis who leave the country, but the actual numbers aren't as important as the reasons that stand behind it. Olim leave because it is difficult to "make it" in Israel—financially, socially, and culturally. Equally important is the fact that Israelis, who were born and who grew up within "the system," leave Israel seeking a more secure financial future. And the percentages of Israelis, or olim, who leave are part and parcel of parents' counterargument to their children's passionate defense for aliya.

Reframing the "Why"

The stressful dialogue within families surrounding the "Why aliya?" question can be minimized if all participants in the debate admit to some basic premises. If you are considering aliya, it will serve you well to concede that you recognize the risks of aliya. And for parents who are frustrated with their children's idealism, focusing on your children's unrealistic expectations with the age-old adage "We are older and wiser" might not do any good and, in fact, might backfire. At the end of the day, both sides need to feel that they have had their say, even if the decision is to forge ahead with aliya. Aliya is hard enough, and if the road to it is littered with hurt feelings, families tend to wall each other off, and no one benefits from that situation.

The "why" debate is exhausting and often seems like an endless loop with no easy exit ramp. But while the discussions are ongoing, we'd recommend that olim and their families keep in mind the following:

Olim: Internalize and admit to yourself and, better yet, to your parents and your extended family that aliya is harder than you represent. Your parents, family, and friends know olim whose absorption was not successful and can lean on the fact that *sabras* (Israeli-born) leave in droves. Don't give up on your passionate belief in aliya, but temper it with a healthy dose of realism about your adopted homeland. If you can find family or friends who have traveled this road before you, seek their guidance, because they have experience in spades.

Parents: Remind yourself that dreams are what created this country. Herzl's rallying cry was, "If you will it, it is no dream." The State of Israel would not exist were it not for those who dreamed, who believed it was possible, whose arteries flowed with idealism, but who were and remain realistic about our geopolitical challenges. Israeli youth inhale and exhale idealism every single day. David Ben Gurion once said, "Anyone who doesn't believe in miracles is not a realist." We are surrounded by enemies (realism), yet we endure (idealism), and your children choose to reject their life (sometimes an easier one) to become part of a society that subsists on a cocktail of idealism and realism. If you keep these concepts in mind during the "why" debate, it might make you proud that they want to be part of something bigger than themselves.

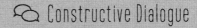 Constructive Dialogue

Olim
"I understand that this will be hard."

Parents
"We might not be able to help with
everything, but please keep us in the loop."

3

The Decision Is Made, Now What?

"Would you tell me, please, which way I ought to go from here?"

—Lewis Carroll, *Alice's Adventures in Wonderland*[1]

Jewish Agency
Known in Hebrew as the Sochnut HaYehudit. In addition to Misrad HaKlita, olim will also face Misrad Hapnim, the Ministry of the Interior, quite early in their aliya

Katin chozer
Someone who received Israeli citizenship in Israel and left before the age of 14

Ezrach chozer
An Israeli citizen born abroad to at least one parent who held Israeli citizenship at the time of birth

Toshav chozer
Citizens of Israel who were 17 or older at the time of returning to Israel, who were considered an Israeli resident in the past, and who resided outside of Israel at least two years

You've gone through the "college" debate; had the circuitous discussion on "why"; and, at some point, started the aliya process. Sometimes, inquiries into aliya were made even before families were told about it. It is even possible that the initial aliya application or portions thereof were submitted before discussions on college or the motives behind aliya.

It doesn't much matter when an official application for aliya was filed but, in most cases, young adults really are looking for implicit or explicit approval or, at the bare minimum, a neutral position from their families. They might complete the entire aliya process without parental approval but, in our view, they are genuinely looking for something that lies between "if it's really what you want" and "we are so proud."

Once the decision is made, the aliya process begins with the *Jewish Agency* and *Misrad HaKlita*. Those making aliya from North America do so solely through Nefesh B'Nefesh. They handle all of the logistical and bureaucratic arrangements, including the interface with government offices. All olim making aliya via Nefesh B'Nefesh are interviewed by Nefesh B'Nefesh; additional interviews are conducted by local Jewish Agency offices. Finally, those making aliya via Nefesh B'Nefesh are assigned a "case worker" or advisor so that they have one person with whom to communicate and ask questions. Those who emigrate from other places around the world continue to process their paperwork through the Jewish Agency and the Ministry of Immigration and Absorption. The paperwork includes, among other things, birth certificates, proof of Judaism, passport, a letter of recommendation, entry and exit forms with dates the oleh entered and exited Israel over seven years, how long each stay was, a health declaration form, a marriage certificate, an FBI background clearance check (for American citizens), and other documents as detailed on the Nefesh B'Nefesh website. No matter where you come from, even if you do not make aliya from a region served through Nefesh B'Nefesh, it is worth checking its website for all of the information needed. If you are approved for aliya, you receive a free one-way ticket to Israel. You can make aliya from inside Israel as well, and the same set of paperwork is required, perhaps with some tweaking.

It is important to note that different rules and rights apply for a katin chozer, ezrach chozer, and toshav chozer. Please make sure to research these issues inasmuch as olim's rights, processes, laws, bureaucratic forms, and more change very frequently and are likely to change over time.

The paperwork process is not complicated, but it is time consuming, and sometimes olim will be asked to resubmit documents that did not sufficiently meet standards. Although the process is not particularly complicated, it can be overwhelming, but it has been so streamlined and simplified that many can handle most, if not all, of it on their own, with the exception perhaps of those who make aliya from within Israel and who don't have easy access to the paperwork they need.

Depending on the age of the olim, there will be a number of decisions facing them immediately. If they are of mandatory draft age, they will receive their tzav rishon, and the IDF miyunim process begins. There are options for mechina k'dam tzva'it, Sherut Leumi, drafting with a group as part of Garin Tzabar, which you must commence in the United States (and not when you arrive in Israel); drafting on your own; and assorted other complex issues that both parents and olim should be aware of and which are addressed in Chapter 7, "IDF/National Service."

Tzav rishon
Initial IDF draft orders received by a recruit

Miyunim
IDF evaluation process to get to your army job

Mechina K'dam Tzva'it
Pre-army academy, a 12- to 18-month program prior to the army that is very Israeli in nature

Sherut Leumi
National Service for those who have an IDF waiver

Garin Tzabar
Group of IDF recruits who make aliya together, live together, and go through the IDF evaluation process together

Ulpan
Hebrew language immersion class, with tests to evaluate levels and progress

Olim who are past mandatory draft age but who have not yet gone to college now have some decisions to make. *Ulpan,* Hebrew immersion class, is a necessity in most cases. It will be fully funded by the government for a period of time, and it is a crucial element of Israeli absorption. *Ulpans* are located throughout the country, they are easy to locate once you arrive in Israel, and you are likely to have a number of options available to you. *Ulpan* isn't supposed to be easy; there are various levels, and you are tested before and after each level to determine appropriate placement. Don't be surprised if your *ulpan* teacher is not warm and fuzzy. We suppose that this is intended to get olim used to the rough and tumble life in Israel. There are entire campuses dedicated to *ulpan* learning. They are soft landing pads, with dormitory-style communal living, and they become social ecosystems for new olim. You will always remember who was in your *ulpan* class, and they will be part of your network forever.

For those who explore colleges in Israel, there are a few English-speaking ones—for example, the Inter-Disciplinary Center (IDC), Hebrew University's Rothberg School, and Bar Ilan University. All have both undergraduate and graduate programs for international students. These institutions offer English-only degree-granting programs, but such programs are few and far between. Simply put, Hebrew is a necessity at any college in Israel—period.

It is rare for olim, regardless of age, to secure employment prior to arriving in Israel. If they contact a potential employer prior to aliya, chances are great that they will be told to "call us when you get here." Olim who don't need to draft into the IDF will be looking for a community that suits them; a local *ulpan;* and, on arrival, employment. For a period of time, they can be financially cushioned by the "absorption basket," which offers monetary support over the first six months. It bears repeating that the Nefesh B'Nefesh website has a plethora of information about all of these issues, along with detailed explanations of olim benefits and rights.

Olim who come with young families have to make educational choices appropriate for them. We took the time to spend a pilot year here and enrolled our children in local schools, and it gave us the ability to make a more informed decision once we made aliya. A pilot year isn't an option for every family; for this reason, we thought it might be helpful to outline some of the educational choices facing olim in Chapter 10, "Coming with Kids."

Some olim handle their own aliya paperwork, decide on IDF service, find a place to live, and enroll their children in educational frameworks—all sans discussion or consultation with their parents or families "back home." Others might selectively choose what to tell their parents but might not seek any advice. Even if olim consult parents or family members or seek guidance, the entire aliya process can be done without much parental input.

The relationship between olim and their families during the planning process depends on the tone of prior discussions on the subject of aliya. Olim who feel like they have been heard, even without the glowing encouragement they were counting on, might feel that the lines of communication are open enough to discuss the aliya process sans judgment. Those whose journeys to date have been plagued by bad feelings, expressions of disappointment, or accusations of abandonment will not likely seek their parents' help with any part of their process. And the converse is true. Parents who believe that their advice was not heeded or that their children are deserting them might refuse to offer any help.

⤺ The Dialogue

Conversations between parents and olim during the application and planning process might sound something like this:

Oleh   Parents

"Do you happen to know where my birth certificate is?"

"Here is the hospital copy we have."
(Hospital copies are not sufficient for the aliya application.)

"I submitted the birth certificate you gave me, but I need an official copy. How do I do that?"

"You wanted to do this; I suggest you figure it out by yourself."

"I need proof of Judaism. Can you call the rabbi for me?"

"Here is the e-mail. You can contact him directly."

"I have to submit a supporting statement describing myself, why I want to make aliya, and what my post-aliya plans are. Can you read mine and tell me what you think?"

"We really didn't understand why you wanted to make aliya to begin with, and we definitely can't attest to the soundness of your post-aliya plan."

"I will be going through the IDF. Just letting you know."

"You understand that it is not all that glorious, right?"

"Education for my kids will cost me less than I pay today."

"Your kids always needed a little more help. How do you plan on taking care of that? And you know that you make less money in Israel."

The reflections above might be exaggerated, and these conversations may take unexpected twists and turns.

We asked olim and parents a series of questions to better understand their communications, or how they perceived them, once the aliya decision was made but before arrival in Israel.

We first asked olim and parents the extent to which they openly discussed the "next steps" of their aliya. The next steps were defined as the application process, the IDF, National Service, university, or places to live. The data in Figure 1 shows that parents have a much stronger view of how much decision making was shared with them after their children decided to make aliya.

Figure 1: Once the aliya decision was made, olim and parents openly discussed the next steps.

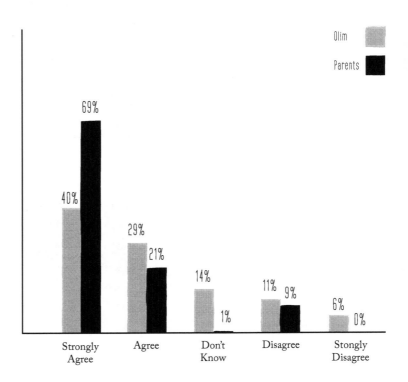

As noted in Figure 1, about 40% of olim strongly agreed that they discussed the "next steps," compared to nearly 70% of parents—a 30% gap, which tends to show that parents believe they were consulted more than they actually were.

Despite this gap, olim and parents seem to hold the view that their discussions about aliya were largely productive (Figure 2).

Figure 2: All along, aliya discussions were frustrating

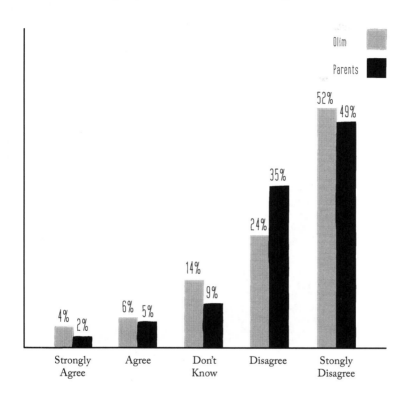

As noted in Figure 2, overwhelming percentages of olim (76%) and parents (84%) strongly disagree/disagree that their aliya discussions were frustrating. We purposefully asked the question in the negative to see whether it elicited strong responses, and it did, leading us to believe that olim and parents perceived their aliya discussions to be productive, or at least not frustrating.

To dig deeper into this issue, we asked whether aliya discussions were limited because they were frustrating, and here too the data clearly shows widespread disagreement with this sentiment (Figure 3).

Figure 3: Aliya discussions between parents and olim were limited because they became frustrating

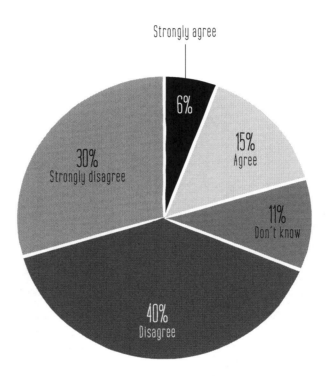

Figure 3 confirms that an overwhelming percentage (70%) disagree or strongly disagree that discussions about aliya were limited because they were frustrating—in other words, neither side limited the discussions because the topic was too aggravating.

We first see a difference between parents and olim when we asked the same question but with an "understanding" quotient, to wit, to what extent were aliya discussions limited because neither side understood the other (Figure 4)?

Figure 4: Aliya discussions between parents and olim were limited because neither side understood the other

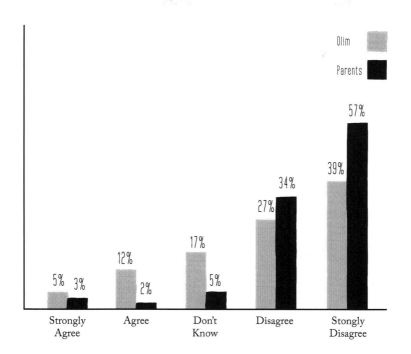

The data in Figure 4 tends to show an "understanding gap." Parents strongly disagreed that aliya conversations were limited because of a lack of understanding (57%) compared to 39%. We view this data as demonstrating that parents are far more certain of their understanding than their children.

When looking at the data in totality, both olim and parents say that communications about post-aliya issues were open and productive, but the olim don't go as far as the parents do. This is a common theme across the entire set of survey questions, where parents are more satisfied than olim with these generative discussions.

⊘ Reality Check

The reality is that aliya and the immediate post-aliya decision period are stressful times with completely unknown territory that lies ahead for olim and the families they are about to leave behind. The older the olim, the more likely they can get through the application process and create post-aliya plans on their own. The younger they are, the more they might need some help from parents to get through the paperwork, and this is more so the case for those making aliya from Israel because they need to have some official documents delivered from their parents overseas. Either way, the entire aliya process is relatively transparent, seamless, and accommodating such that even young olim can sail through it largely alone. It does not, however, mean that they should do it without keeping their parents informed. Young families who make aliya would do well by coming on a pilot trip to scope out communities and schools that are appropriate for them or, at the bare minimum, be prepared to move from their "landing place" if it doesn't suit them after a period of time. In fact, we recommend that you "try out" certain communities and schools before you settle on one.

▢ Reframing the "Now What?"

Immigration to Israel starts a geographical separation from the only unconditional support system children have ever known. It is admirable and important for olim to try and accomplish as much as they can on their own. Yet, if olim summon the courage to ask for parental or other familial help or advice, parents ought to try and put their feelings aside and offer some guidance. "Guide" does not mean "complete on behalf of." Neither parents nor olim really understand how complicated aliya is or how complex the choices really are, which means neither group is steeped in knowledge about any issue. Therefore, once the aliya application, planning process, and post-aliya plans begin to take shape, we recommend that olim and their parents keep the following in mind:

Olim: Take into consideration that your gain, defined as your first steps toward Israeli citizenship, is the beginning of your parent's loss, a course that will put many kilometers and time zones between you. If you have children, your parents now understand that they will be far away as their grandchildren grow up in Israel. You *finally* took the first steps toward becoming an Israeli citizen and you are excited, eager, exhilarated, and filled with anticipation for your soon-to-be new life. No one suggests that you should moderate how you feel. Keeping your parents in the loop, regardless of whether you need their help, can combat their feelings of isolation and detachment. You never know when your parents have a connection that you might need down the road. Keeping your parents at arm's length can ultimately prevent you from receiving information that could be of assistance to you.

Parents: Acknowledging your sense of loss once the aliya process has begun is perfectly reasonable. Once the deed is done, you might need to accept your children's decision no matter how hard it is or how wrong-headed you believe it is. Even if you gave your complete blessing, be prepared to be left out of the loop during the application process. If your children don't keep you updated, it's acceptable to ask where things stand. Avoiding it won't postpone the inevitable. If your assistance or advice is sought, answers like, "I didn't ask for this, so don't come to me," can be construed as resenting a decision made without your consent. If we are honest with ourselves, there are likely to be a slew of decisions our children make with which we take serious issue, regardless of aliya. This is just the start of decisions they will make without your input, and they are far more likely to consult you in the years ahead if they get the impression that you can disagree without being disagreeable.

⬭ Constructive Dialogue

Olim
"I am not sure I can do it all myself. Can I come to you if I need help?"

Parents
"If you run into a problem, let's try to solve it together."

4

The Airport: A Gateway To A New Life

"Today's Special Moments Are Tomorrow's Memories"

—The Genie, Disney Movie Aladdin[1]

Teudat zehut
Identity card with unique number that everyone must carry, with a small piece of paper called a "sefach" that identifies your first level relationships, which must be changed at the Ministry of Interior when you undergo lifecycle events— like births or marriage

Lift
Container sent by cargo ship. Israelis call a lift a "container," and it sounds like "con-tay-ner"

Over the course of a few months (sometimes as little as a month, depending on how organized the oleh is), a prospective oleh completed the paperwork and was interviewed by the appropriate authorities, and the State of Israel approved the request to become a citizen. Whether the aliya process is done through Nefesh B'Nefesh or the Jewish Agency, all olim who immigrate from outside of Israel receive a one-way free ticket to Israel. You become a citizen on arrival at Ben Gurion Airport. All olim are directed to the airport's second floor to the Ministry of Immigration. They sign some more paperwork; receive the first payment from their absorption basket in cash; and are handed their *teudat zehut,* a blue card that sits within a blue case and that includes the words to the national anthem "Hatikva" (The Hope).

What precedes all this excitement is the packing and ultimately parting ways at the airport. Young olim will not likely have much in terms of possessions, and even though they are entitled to a *lift* shipped to Israel, they might not have enough to justify the expense. There is a common misconception that the lift is free. It is not. Shipping to Israel does incur costs but, as an oleh, much of what you import to the country will be tax free. There are some exceptions, and there are some items that are simply not economical to ship, particularly if they require importing replacement parts or paying for service when there are no expert servicemen in Israel.[2] Most young olim will be able to bring their prized possessions without shipping on a lift. Parents, family, and friends should be prepared to bring items with them when they come to visit, and that is an arrangement that can go on forever. We still do it.

For olim who travel on a Nefesh B'Nefesh flight and who live near one of the airports where Nefesh B'Nefesh operates, the only "trip" to be made is from home to the airport to meet up with Nefesh B'Nefesh officials. Others might have to take another domestic flight to meet up with a Nefesh B'Nefesh flight. Nefesh B'Nefesh flights, either charter or group, come with some level of fanfare. Those who board a flight without Nefesh B'Nefesh do so without any ceremony.

The run up to the departing flight is by far the most emotional time for olim and their families, regardless of age. In the weeks prior to boarding that plane, olim, their parents, and their extended families often experience diametrically opposed sentiments. Olim brim with excitement and enthusiasm, and parents are mostly filled with a sense of sadness, isolation, and dread, sometimes mixed with pride.

If you watch Nefesh B'Nefesh ceremonies online (they are all archived on their YouTube channel), you will see parents hugging their children and blessing them, with tears streaming down their faces. Broadcasts include positive emotions and statements of pride, feelings that don't make viewers feel uncomfortable. Naturally, these broadcasts don't include outright expressions of disappointment or disapproval of an oleh's choice. Nor do they include interviews with parents or close family members who actively chose not to accompany their children to the airport. The idea is to broadcast a "feel-good" vibe, acknowledging that this is a momentous occasion.

Rabbi Yehoshua Fass, Co-Founder and Executive Director of Nefesh B'Nefesh, says it best. There are many welcoming moments for olim when they arrive in Israel. There is a grand and moving arrival ceremony. There is the moment when your neighbors realize you just arrived. Teachers; doctors; postal office workers; and, yes, even cab drivers will welcome you. Many "hellos" but only one opportunity for goodbye, these precious hours spent at the airport before your loved one boards a plane to start a new life.

The emotional ramifications of "Aliya Day" probably reflect the nature of the relationship between olim and their parents and the manner in which they related to one another in the run up to aliya. Parents who have been ardent Zionists up until that point might sound far less so at this time. Even if parents gave their wholehearted support for aliya, it does not negate the emotions that take place when it comes time to say farewell. We also note that there is an entire absorption system in Israel that "hugs" every oleh. But families left behind go home alone, without a structure to "hug" them when they return in tears.

⌬ The Dialogue

Yerida
The Hebrew word for "to decline," Yerida is the opposite of aliya, "to rise up"

Perhaps olim are grateful or relieved that they have survived the trial by fire known as their parents' or family's "interrogation" that preceded this day. And perhaps parents have assuaged their fears by thinking that aliya is temporary and reversible, and it is. *Yerida,* leaving Israel and rescinding citizenship, is not as hard as it might sound. Less paperwork is required to leave than it is to become a citizen. And it is doable with little ramifications, certainly after the first three years.

We asked both parents and olim about the departure on Aliya Day. We were primarily interested in hearing the emotional stories from olim and parents in those moments prior to parting. As noted in Figure 1, more than two-thirds of olim in our survey, 67%, indicated that they were accompanied by their parents to the airport when they left for Israel. A total of 23% indicated that they were not escorted by parents, either because they made aliya from within Israel (13%), or it was logistically impossible to be with one another right before the flight to Israel (10%) i.e., they lived too far away from the airport where the official departure took place. Only 10% of olim respondents indicated that they traveled to the airport without their parents when they made aliya.

Figure 1: Percentage of olim accompanied by parents to the airport

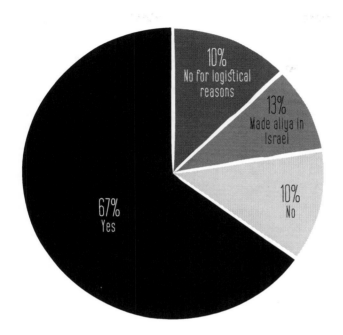

The more interesting and emotional data came from the open-ended questions asking parents and olim to describe the nature of the departure at the airport. More than 35% of respondents answered this question, and over 90% of those respondents indicated that their aliya day was emotional. Of the details reported, we attempted to understand the differences between olim and their parents. Due to the free flow of the answers, it is difficult to statistically code them, but we were able to discern certain patterns in the data.

Figure 2 shows that both parents and olim expressed sadness at the time of departure, although in many cases olim indicated that their sadness came from the fact that their aliya was the cause of their parents' sadness. Of the parents who were sad, one third of them were also either happy or proud, demonstrating the mixed feelings that parents have on that day.

The significant differences can be seen when one isolates the "happy/excited" factor. Here, nearly 3 times as many olim expressed excitement than parents did. When olim expressed positive feelings, they primarily indicated excitement, and when parents expressed positive feelings, their emotion was reflected as pride, a more natural emotional for parents in general.

Figure 2: Aliya day expressed emotions

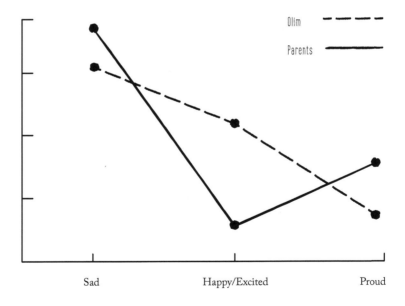

A little over 10% of respondents reported diametrically opposed views: sad parents on the one hand and excited olim on the other (Figure 3). In only 5% of the cases did olim and parents both report only positive feelings without reporting sadness.

Figure 3: Percentage of diametrically opposed emotions

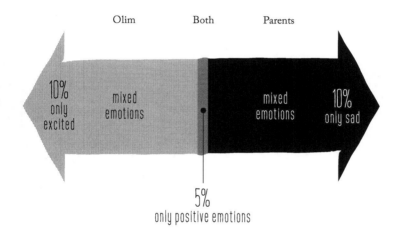

Even though our aliya was more than eleven years ago, we were very moved by the comments from parents and olim. Of the hundreds of responses we received, we selected a few that demonstrate the dichotomy between olim and their parents on Aliya Day. Minor changes were made to protect the identity of respondents. Words like "emotional," "sad," "excited," "nervous," "difficult," "anxious," "heart-wrenching," "hard," "pride," and "teary," were woven through many of the responses, some of which are included on the next two pages (Figure 4):

Figure 4: Survey of the language/emotions expressed by olim and parents at the airport

What Olim Said

"My parents were holding back tears. I was excited but my sister was the proudest of all."

"Fear of the unknown and excitement on my part. Extreme sadness for my parents and grandparents."

"My parents stayed on the security line with me 45 minutes. My Mom said that she was so proud of me for doing this. My Dad said that, worst case scenario, I could always come home and live with them. They called me 10 minutes after I went through security to confirm that I still wanted to do this and to wish me luck."

"It was emotional for my parents but I was more excited for the future than anything else."

"I was excited and nervous. My parents put up a strong front but I found out that they cried as soon as I got through security at the airport."

"I remember I cried, and I never cried leaving my parents. Ever. I was glad they saw me off."

"My Mom wore sunglasses. She was bawling. They surprised me in Israel one week later."

"My parents were crying but trying to smile, and I felt very emotional about leaving them, feeling the pain I was causing them and the magnitude of the decision."

⌯ What Parents Said

"I had mixed feelings. Happy for him following his dreams, but worried about his career prospects and missing being together."

"For me a very difficult day. I understand that he needed to do this. I didn't know at that point when we would be able to see each other again and we don't have family in Israel."

"Joyous and sad at the same time."

"I experienced many emotions: pride, sadness, loss, excited, worried. I cried a lot that day and for many days after."

"It was sad but we were hopeful that this would be a successful start to a new chapter of life that would be rewarding and life affirming."

"Our child had chosen his path with reluctant agreement from us and was about to begin the military."

"It was very special to us that our child was taking such a bold stand and was willing to give up so much for her values. It was very hard to say goodbye, but we were proud."

"It felt like open heart surgery without the anesthesia."

⌀ Reality Check

The reality is that every family dynamic is different, and that is certainly the case when it comes to the parent-child relationship. As one can see, the reactions on Aliya Day vary widely. But one way or the other, we guarantee it will be emotional.[3] The value of that airport departure will remain an ingrained memory for the rest of your life, and our advice, quite simply, is to treat that moment as one that all family members, particularly parent and child, can remember for its poignancy.

☐ Reframing the Airport Departure

In our case, one set of parents lived too far away to be present at the airport, so we traveled to say goodbye a week earlier. Another set of parents lived a few kilometers from the airport, yet one parent simply was emotionally unable to enter the airport and the other was too emotional to stay for the Nefesh B'Nefesh ceremony, let alone until we passed through security. Our daughter's friends were present, and we have pictures of them crying together on the floor. One couple who made aliya before us had been visiting New York at the time, and another, good friends who lived five houses away from us, came to the airport to see us off. It was a mix of support and overwhelming sadness at the same time. Single olim vs. married ones with children might have different experiences with parents/grandparents at the airport, but either circumstance is rife with a range of feelings. Everyone involved will remember this day for a long time to come, and it would be nice if it could be remembered without resentment, but to do it, here are some concepts to keep in mind:

Olim: Soften or temper your enthusiasm for your as-yet untainted Israeli life so that your parents don't get the impression that you are excited to be released from their control. You likely don't feel that way anyway but, on some level, your exhilaration can unwittingly cause your parents to perceive you as insensitive or callous toward their emotional state at the time. You might not be aware of it at that moment, but the time will come, we hope very far into the future, when you will feel incredibly torn as your parents age, and only then will you begin to understand the helplessness your parents felt at this very moment. Once you arrive in Israel, pace yourself. Your first year will be a hazy mix of euphoria, grueling adjustment, and #OnlyInIsrael moments—good ones and bad ones.

Parents: Resist the urge for a guilt trip because the time will come, we hope very far into the future, when guilt will come of its own volition, as your children try to juggle families, careers, and their deep-seated desire to be with you when you need them. On this day, if you part ways in a manner that is filled with judgment, it will likely be hard for your children to voluntarily connect with you post-aliya because they will assume that every move will be viewed negatively. There is nothing you can say or do now that will stop this ship from sailing, so draw on your inner strength to make it as positive as you can. Go ahead and cry. Accept without judgment that your child might not cry. And, as hard as it is, tell them you are proud; reiterate that you will always be there for them no matter what; and be the very last thing they see as they pass through the point of no return at the airport, even if they want to shake you as hard as they can. Then pace yourself for the long post-aliya marathon that lies ahead.

Constructive Dialogue

Olim
"I will miss you."

Parents
"I will miss you."

5

Out There on Their Own: Health Care, Banks, Credit Cards, Contracts & Apartments

"And the choices we make are ultimately our own responsibility."

-Eleanor Roosevelt[1]

Once an oleh arrives in Israel, the process of daily life begins. Nefesh B'Nefesh issues a step-by-step guide on what logistically ought to be done, and we encourage a deep dive on its website to find information on all these topics. Every topic in this chapter can be summarized in one sentence: If you aren't sure how to navigate it or have no idea where to start, or if you get stuck somewhere in the process, please ask an Israeli—perhaps a long-term oleh or an Israeli friend from work. It will go a long way to have an ad hoc advisor who speaks the language or has been through these systems. A few general points to be made about each issue before we delve into their impact on young olim and their parents:

Health Care

Kupat holim
The socialized medicine single payer system-choose the strongest in your area and you can switch plans every quarter

There are four major health insurance plans, *kupat holim,* in Israel's socialized medicine single-payer system. Every public health insurance plan offers supplemental "add-ons" that can include, for instance, the ability to see a private doctor a few times a year for reimbursement up to a certain percentage, coverage of certain medications that are not covered in the *Misrad HaBriyut* basket for drug coverage, and more. There is a growing private health insurance market in Israel, but explore each one with insurance agents before committing to one.

Misrad HaBriyut
Ministry of Health

Your *rofeh mishpacha* is the key to the entire health care system, including securing referrals to specialists. Olim would be wise to find one that is fluent in English so that there is no stress over this issue. Patients must be far more proactive about their health than they need to be in other countries. It is not a criticism of doctors per se but a burdened socialized medicine system. All insurance plans are highly digitized with useful mobile applications. While there might be English versions, they

Rofeh mishpacha
Primary care physician

are not as fully developed; for this reason, command of Hebrew will allow fullest usage of this technology. As uncomfortable as it is, it is best to learn to navigate the health care system in Hebrew, regardless of the fact that doctors do speak English. The words *hafnaya, hitchayvut,* and *mirsham* are fairly crucial words because they are part of the health care flow process that looks something like this:

Hafnaya
Referral

Hitchayvut
*Commit-
ment to pay*

Mirsham
Prescription

Figure 1: The basic medical care process

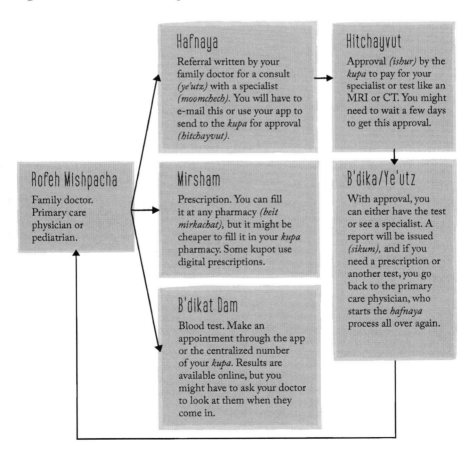

Bank Accounts

Amalot
Bank charges such as transaction costs and monthly fees

Amalot, bank charges, are an enigma even to most Israelis, and to try and understand or fight these charges can be maddening. Laws governing banks can change, and some of us have just stopped trying to understand it all, chalking it up to the cost of living in Israel. All American citizens are required to complete a W9 form as well as FACTA, an international banking disclosure requirement.

Minus
Pronounced "mee-noose" in Hebrew, a monthly overdraft

While online banking has improved drastically over the years, a command of Hebrew will be necessary to use it. Banks automatically allow you to have a certain monthly overdraft, known as *minus.* This is quite a frightening statement for many who did not know it in advance or for parents to whom this will be a completely foreign and dangerous concept. The difficulty in carrying monthly costs against your salary is the motivation behind overdraft allowances for up to a certain amount. The Central Bureau of Statistics reports that 42% of families in 2018 were in overdraft at least one month in the previous year. Half of them reported that this is their "general situation" and that they were in overdraft 10 months in the past year.[2]

Kartis ashra'i
Credit card

Credit Cards

Tashlumim
Payment plan to spread out payments, normally without "ribit" (interest)

A *kartis ashra'i,* a credit card, is really a debit card and is connected to your bank account. There are certain limits placed on the amount that can be charged to that credit card monthly, and it is generally tied to your salary. It is not that difficult to increase your "credit line" so that you can charge more per month. You are frequently offered the opportunity to charge a purchase in *tashlumim,* which essentially spreads a charge over a number of months, and every Israeli does it. If you use *tashlumim*, you really never have a handle on how much you've spent on your credit card in any given month, unless you are constantly looking at your credit card statement. Try as best you can to budget yourself and avoid too many *tashlumim*.

Contracts

Cell phones and apartments (and other services like home Internet) are usually "relationships" defined by a *chozeh,* a contract. The cost of cell phone service in Israel has gone down dramatically, and you can jump from company to company usually after a year. Cell phones themselves, however, remain pricey. WhatsApp, FB Messenger, FaceTime, and Telegram via WiFi enable international calling with no extra cost, but there are Israeli phone companies that will provide you with a virtual international phone number so your friends and family overseas can call your cell from a local number. Cell phone contracts are standardized and there isn't much negotiation on the language, but there are companies that offer contracts in English.

Chozeh
Contract of any kind.

Apartments

Over the years, the logistics behind apartment hunting have become easier thanks to social media groups. Most single olim will likely rent an apartment together or will join an apartment that already has other roommates.

Apartments in Israel often lack some basic appliances that would otherwise be part of a rental in other parts of the world, like ovens, refrigerators, stovetops, washing machines, dryers, and air-conditioners. Items purchased by a tenant can move with them. Bed frames, mattresses, closets, desks, tables, and other items will have to be purchased as well. While appliances and other household items are generally not prohibitively expensive, young olim tend to skimp on what they perceive as conveniences to save on costs, like foregoing a standard oven in exchange for a toaster oven, or a dryer in exchange for the sun. It is understandable that young people tend to make do with very little; however, you can circumvent austere and spartan living arrangements by joining Facebook groups and Facebook marketplace, where you can buy used items at reasonable prices.

Certain household appliances might not be expensive to purchase but can be expensive to run. For example, most dryers in Israel are electric and they are not particularly expensive. However, electricity costs in Israel are high, and the electric bill (sent every two months) is often the most expensive household utility (after local property taxes known as *arnona*). Running an electric dryer is expensive, but the purchase of it is less so. Gas dryers are available, but they are expensive to purchase and most apartments need a special gas line installed to run them. Air-conditioning units are also expensive to run, but considering the length of the summer, some might simply purchase one and take it with them when they move.

When looking at apartments, be on the lookout for bathrooms without windows. They can get moldy. Look to see if there is gas running into the apartment—not everyone has it, which means everything runs on electric, and that can be expensive. Look for stains on the walls or peeling paint, a sure sign that there were leaks in the apartment. To be honest, we have yet to know anyone who hasn't experienced some sort of leak from the rain. Outdoor space, even a tiny porch, is crucial for your mental health. Apartments are small, and you won't like being cooped up. Take a look at the electric panel to see if it is one phase or two or three. If it's one phase, be aware that

Arnona
Local property taxes paid to the municipality, a cost passed on by landlords to renters who pay it monthly in addition to rent

running two appliances can blow the electricity. Run the hot water in the middle of the day to make sure the *dood* gives you hot water. Finally, it always helps to have someone else look at the apartment as a second set of eyes.

Apartment leases were the subject of regulatory reform a few years ago. For a long period of time, apartment owners increased rents at unreasonable rates (because they could), failed to offer certain basic amenities like a working bathroom (because they could), refused to make reasonable repairs (because they could), and demanded high-priced security deposits or guarantees (because they could). While the law has changed, we have seen more than our fair share of contracts that we would not necessarily agree to and, in some cases, we were able to secure more reasonable conditions when we had an opportunity to see leases before they were signed.

Nearly all olim will encounter a landlord who will want their tenants to find an *arev,* someone who guarantees that they will honor the terms of the lease if the tenant does not. Most landlords will not accept a guarantor who isn't Israeli, so parents' guarantees won't help if they live outside Israel. We have been guarantors for a few olim, and we largely felt comfortable doing so because we knew the overseas parents stood by their children and would honor their children's commitments. The agreement to become a guarantor is a highly personal one, and one that parents ought to be aware of. If they have friends in Israel, they will come in handy as guarantors.

All rental contracts require some sort of *pikadon,* a security deposit to cover damage to the apartment that might be discovered after the lease is up. The law today does not allow any more than three months' rent for this security deposit. The landlord might also ask for *hafkadat check patuach,* open checks to the water, gas, and electric companies should you finish the lease without paying the last bit of utility bills. Make sure

Dood
Water tank on the roof, usually heated by solar panels

Arev
Guarantor

Pikadon
Deposit, in this case some kind of security deposit to protect property

Hafkadat check patuach
An open check (with no amount indicated) that is signed, in this context, for utilities

that all contracts include provisions for returning the security deposit and the open utility checks when the lease is over.

Most, if not all, of the above issues will be handled by olim without parental consultation. By nature, communications between olim and family members dwindle on arrival in Israel. Time zone differences and the fact that Israel's Friday is equivalent to the rest of the world's Sunday (a workday for Israelis) narrows the communication window. Regardless, parents are hardly in a position to assist, considering the geographic distance, language barriers, and cultural gaps.

Our survey (Figure 2) shows that olim and parents seem to overcome time zone or geographic challenges, for both olim and parents indicated that their post-aliya communication occurs at least once a week via WhatsApp, FB Messenger,

Figure 2: Post aliya communications between parents and olim that took place at least once a week

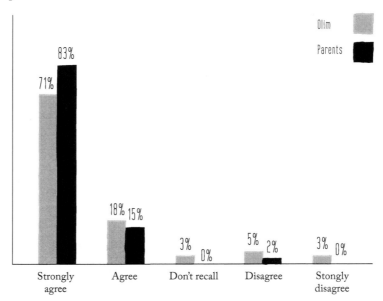

Skype, Telegram, phone calls or emails.

Nearly all parents (98%) strongly agree/agree that post-aliya communication takes place at least weekly and nearly 90% of olim (89%) share the same sentiment, suggesting that the "connection" is important to both groups and that the wide variety of communication media helps to increase the frequency of contact.

Yet the frequency of communication does not necessarily mean that olim consult with their parents on important post-aliya issues. When it comes to discussions about post-aliya official documents, our survey shows that olim and parents mostly agree with one another that consultation occurred on some issues but not others. More significantly, the data (Figure

Figure 3: Following aliya, the oleh consulted with parents prior to signing official documents

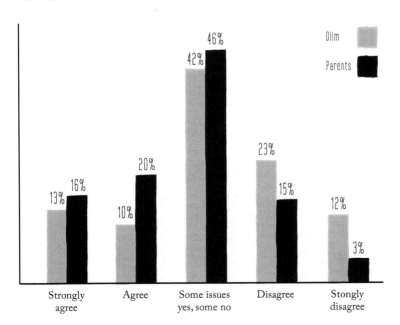

3) tends to show that parents think they are being consulted more often (36% of parents agree/strongly agree) when olim represent that they are not (35% strongly disagree/disagree).

Similar responses were seen in a question about post aliya monetary issues (Figure 4.) About 87% of parents believe that their children discuss monetary issues with them (often or occasionally), compared to 69% of olim. One can read the data as supporting the notion that olim consult with parents with

Figure 4: When monetary issues arose after aliya, how often were there discussions between the oleh and a parent?

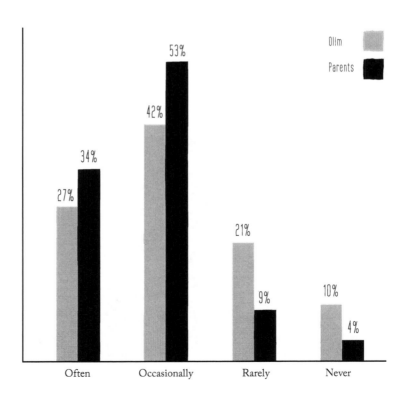

some regularity about monetary issues, but not quite as much as parents believe. About 31% of olim report that they rarely or never discuss monetary issues with their parents, compared to 13% of parents.

We applaud the fact that parents and olim communicate as frequently as they do, for it is unquestionably important. It would be even better if olim would consult with their parents more regularly on post-aliya issues or monetary concerns.

The Dialogue

There is no doubt that within the first year or two of aliya, there are many experiences that are new, and many of us find official documents and contracts daunting. Sales representatives and government institutions often don't have the patience or the time to allow us to wade through a Hebrew document, and we find ourselves just signing them, assuming that it will be alright. Sometimes it is not, and olim might find themselves complaining to parents about an issue, seeking some level of sympathy. The conversation can go something like this:

Oleh   Parents

"My cell phone/Internet company just
increased its rates without even telling me."

"Didn't you read the contract before you
signed it?"

"I keep on complaining that the fuse blows
in our apartment, and the landlord won't
fix it."

"Don't you have rights? Didn't you read the
contract before you signed it?"

**Hora'at
keva**
*Automatic
monthly
wire
transfer*

"I can't cancel my *"hora'at keva,"* so they
keep on taking money out of my account."

"Don't you know how to cancel the charge?
Didn't you read the paperwork?"

"I have to wait six months for an MRI."

"Why can't you just pay for it privately?"

"It's like this for everyone in Israel. You just
don't understand Israel."

"If everyone jumped off the Brooklyn
Bridge, would you follow? Just explain to
me why it is like this."

Every one of these concerns can often boil down to a combination of a few issues: failure to read a contract or official document before signing, an aversion to consulting an Israeli about the implications, and a genuine cultural divide between the way Israel and the rest of the world works.

☑ Reality Check

The reality is that within a year after aliya, parents and families "back home" will start to hear the refrain "you just don't understand Israel" on these and many other issues. Cultural differences and practices are indeed vast. But the experiences olim have in these areas are their rights of passage. Renting a subpar apartment for too much money, or one that lacked the very basic of amenities, will have taught them a lesson. It is all part and parcel of their assertion of their rights, understanding what they "get" before they sign, and asking someone more experienced for help. Even we did.

☐ Reframing Your New Life

Olim need to know whom to ask for help; know when to ask; and, most importantly, have the courage to do so. Our data shows that they communicate often enough with their parents, yet shy away from consulting with parents about post-aliya issues or financial challenges. A faraway parent can do little to assist, and olim might have to struggle through this growth period on their own. Yet there are some concepts that both parties can keep in mind:

Olim: Ask for help. Find appropriate Facebook groups, join them, and solicit advice from others. Know your rights, and if you don't, ask for assistance. People are more than willing to help you with just about anything. There are rights-based organizations with hotlines, e-mails, and even WhatsApp groups to answer questions, so don't be afraid to reach out. Your first apartment will be an experience—and not necessarily a good one. You might have signed contracts that took advantage of you, but you won't repeat this mistake twice. Next time, ask someone with more experience to take a look at the contract or a potential apartment before you agree to anything. Find a primary care physician who literally "speaks your language" because when you are under the weather, your basic Hebrew skills will not be enough to understand how to navigate the system. Get to know what *Terem* or other after-hour clinics do, because they can be good options in semi-emergency situations at night. If you don't like your community, seek out another one before you plant more permanent roots.

Terem
Usually a 24-hour urgent care clinic with a financial arrangement with a kupa so that your fee is minimal

Parents: At this point in your child's aliya, your due diligence replaces your powerlessness. Just because you can't help doesn't mean you stop asking questions. Don't give up on attentiveness, and while you might be perceived as "interfering," you are better off asking than waiting for them to volunteer information. Your child might not be happy about the intervention, but better safe than sorry. One area deserves vigilance, and that's health care. Olim might not be forthcoming about their health because they think it is not all that relevant or helpful to involve you. Nevertheless, be alert and, over time, if you have reason to believe that they have been under the weather for too long, contact friends in Israel who might be able to step in.

Constructive Dialogue

Olim
"I am not sure I understand the system for [fill in the blank]."

Parents
"We can reach out to someone who can help you get through it."

6

Friends and Family, and Friends Who Become Family

"I'll be there for you, when the rain starts to pour,
I'll be there for you, like I've been there before."

—The Rembrandts[1], theme song from the television series Friends

Some olim arrive in Israel without a single Israeli family member or friend who preceded them to Israel. They are literally and figuratively alone. Others might have aunts, uncles, close cousins, distant cousins, friends of the family, or even siblings who preceded them on aliya and who become part of their support system. There are also situations where olim have family or friends in Israel, yet they seem to be shy or unwilling to reach out. Even when olim have family or friends to lean on, there is a good chance that they will make new friends who will become their new family and their support network.

Concepts like "family" and "support system" take on a whole new meaning in Israel. Whether they are actual blood relatives, friends of parents, parents of friends, or a growing circle of olim in their late 20s or early 30s with an expanding network of their own, these are crucial relationships. They are the lynchpin for olim, names parents will hear over and over and who host olim over holidays or Shabbat.

It is worth noting that all Jewish holidays are mostly national holidays in Israel. Even among the nonreligious, holidays of all kinds, including Friday nights, are family time, and young olim can find themselves alone in a country where restaurants, bars, movie theaters, and even public transportation largely close down. They are invited, or invite themselves, to anyone who is considered part of their support system and whom they now consider family by blood or by association.

It might take some time before parents understand the rhythms of Israeli life, and they might not know to ask where olim are spending the holidays or Shabbat. But it is important to pay attention to the recurring hosts, because those are the families or friends who can become a potential resource for parents.

Young adults are not inclined to volunteer details of their leisure or weekend activities with parents. To the contrary, these are precisely the years when parents are likely to receive less information from their children, not more.

Many olim have "new families" that they create. It can be a friend from work who becomes your close confidante on employment matters who transforms into an adopted sister. It can be an Israeli neighbor who will help demystify your utility bill. Or it can be an oleh who has been here for decades who will regale you with stories about how much harder it was "back then."

No matter how you find these amazing people, they become your adopted family—the person within the same time zone, and maybe even a few blocks away, to whom you can turn for immediate advice. As olim, we tend to come without a nuclear family, and so we create our own. As one of our survey respondents noted, "Find yourself a way to get an adopted family even before coming to Israel, someone who will invite you over for Shabbat, who can give advice on rentals, who connects you to Israelis. Try to connect with actual people before coming." In essence, build your "family" in Israel because they will become the people you lean on in good times and bad and more likely for day-to-day living.

Becoming an adopted family is a responsibility. It can mean more than a meal or doing the laundry for a soldier. If olim turn to you for assistance, it is because they need help, and while an adoptive family's guidance is important, it is equally important to know your limitations and admitting where your own knowledge is lacking.

Young olim often meet their significant other or spouse in Israel, whether it is a native Israeli or another oleh. Opinions abound on whether olim prefer to be in relationships with other olim or, at a bare minimum, those who were born into families speaking the same mother tongue. Other olim might prefer "pure bred" native Israelis because they believe it solidifies them as "true Israelis," justifying their place in the country.

Regardless of whether it is another oleh or a native Israeli, parents of olim in relationships find themselves completely out of the loop, unable to meet the significant other in person perhaps until it is all a "done deal." As parents, if it is important to you to get to know the significant other before the train has left the station, let your children know. They might not honor your request, but at least you will have expressed your opinion that you don't want to be the "last one to know."

Finally, when the time comes for a wedding, it is fair to say that weddings are quite informal events in Israel—no suits, ties, gowns, or high heels. Attendance at these events requires at best a clean white shirt and nice pants or a simple dress. Sometimes it can be jeans and sandals. At weddings, there really isn't anything like "walking down the aisle," because there barely is an aisle at all. People just tend to congregate in a group.

Israeli weddings, like many things in Israel, are sometimes planned at the last minute. Invitations might look quite casual. And it is highly likely that paper invitations will not be mailed—even if they are, the invitations are not likely to get to anyone on time because the Israeli postal service is one of the most unreliable systems in the country. Don't be surprised if weddings are held in a forest or in the desert and food is served informally, buffet style. You will not likely succeed in convincing your children to buck this informal trend. Finally, lingua franca of a wedding (or a celebration of any kind) is Hebrew, which means that speeches and videos might not be in English.

💬 The Dialogue

Parents living thousands of miles away are likely to be seen as micromanagers or interlopers when trying to understand where their children spend their time. The conversation can go something like this:

Parent   Oleh

"Where are you spending the weekend?"

"Friends."

"Who with?"

"Friends."

"Anyone I know?"

"Friends from the army, so no."

"Any plans for Rosh Hashana?"

"Having friends over and been invited out to friends."

You get the drift. We hypothesized that there is a difference between what parents *think* they know and how their children choose to portray it. And the data proved our theory correct.

We asked olim and parents to what extent they know where the olim spend their weekends or holidays, shown in Figure 1.

Most olim (60%) strongly agree/agree that their parents know where they spend their weekends or holidays. More parents (76%) think that they know where their children are, somewhat proving our theory correct—parents think they know more than they do.

Figure 1: Parents know where their olim/children spend their weekends and holidays.

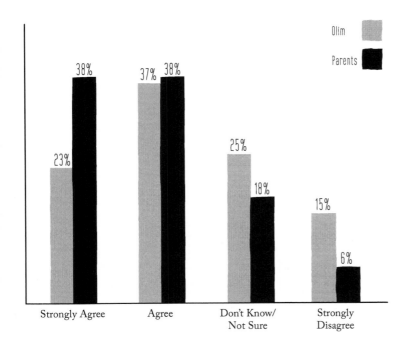

To test how much parents really know about their children's social life in Israel, we asked whether parents were able to name at least two families that olim visit regularly (Figure 2).

Figure 2: Parents can name at least two families that the olim visited regularly (1x/month)

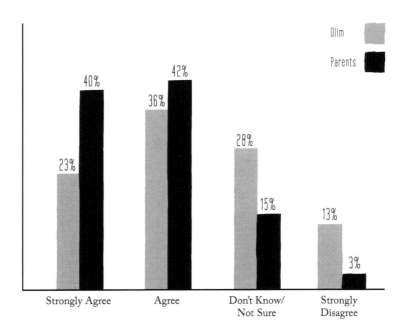

More than 80% of parents report that they can name at least two families the olim visit at least once a month, compared to 59% of olim—nearly the same percentage of olim who think that their parents know where they were, as was asked in the preceding question. And here, too, parents think they know more than they probably do.

☑ Reality Check

The reality is that life can get pretty lonely in a new country, and most olim, regardless of age, want a connection to friends or family in Israel. We all crave familiar connections, and olim are no different. Friends often become family. They are the people who will have more day-to-day contact with olim than parents will, and they tend to know the circumstances facing olim. For this reason, it is helpful if parents develop relationships with their children's Israeli friends or family so that they have someone to consult and figure out how best to assist if necessary. It also gives olim a place to turn as they try to solve some of the logistical issues discussed in Chapter 5.

A word about the concept of families who "adopt" olim. Any oleh can have an adopted family *(mishpacha m'ametzet)*, and there is nothing formal about it. A lone soldier can have an adopted family. A young mother can have an "adopted mother," either an *olah vatika* her own age or an older Israeli as her "go to" resource. The word "adopted" can be a highly charged term without intention. Young olim who talk about their adopted families might not realize that biological parents feel like they have taken a back seat in their children's lives. Even older olim who tell their parents or families that they have an "adopted mom" or an "adopted sister/brother" might unwittingly hurt their biological families, the parents who brought them into the world or siblings who shared a lifetime of experiences. Please know that the use of the term "my adopted family" isn't in lieu of parental ties. It does not replace mothers, fathers, or siblings, and adopted families are not *in loco parentis*. Adopted families will make efforts to keep in touch with biological families, visit each other if possible, and otherwise stay connected—only because it is simply the best way for olim to succeed.

Mishpacha m'ametzet
Adopted family

Olah vatika/oleh vatik
Oleh who has been in Israel a long time

The concept of an adopted family carries with it a tremendous amount of societal clout in Israel. If an adopted mother or father intervenes to help an oleh, being introduced as the adopted family has weight, it has meaning, it is understood by other Israelis, and it garners respect. It allows adopted parents/families to engage with Israeli society on behalf of olim. Israelis will know that an oleh isn't alone; that someone is watching; that they won't allow olim to be taken advantage of; and, more importantly, that they care. Families who adopt olim always respect the place of biological families left behind.

☐ Reframing the Accusations of Interference

**Tafsiki
lachfor**
*Stop digging
or needling
me*

Predictably, young independent olim, the idealistic ones who left an easier life to make room for a harder one, are going to chafe at parental attempts to insert themselves into their personal lives. "Stop micromanaging," they will say or, worse yet, *"tafsiki lachfor,"* Hebrew for "stop digging." Parents can gain some peace of mind if they have a personal resource with whom to consult, despite the olim's irritation at the meddling, and while the interference might offend a young adult, perhaps this should be kept in mind:

Olim: Concede to your parents' need to be connected to your life in Israel. If they want to meet your friends, get to know the people in your life, and network with your support system, let them. It has the potential to help you down the road. You might not have time to solve some sort of problem that arises, but your parents or even extended family might be able to tap into relationships in Israel to help.

Parents: Concede your children's need to be independent. Be assured that you have an "anchor" in Israel in your children's friends or "Israeli family." It will be nearly impossible to keep track of your children all the time. Instead, make do with getting to know one or two of their friends and create relationships that give you a window into your children's world.

⌾ Constructive Dialogue

Olim
"Did I ever tell you about my friend Ido, who was in my course in the army?"

Parents
"We'd love to take your friends out to dinner when we visit."

7

IDF/National Service: I've Asked What I Can Do for My Country

*"Really I feel less keen about the Army every day.
I think the Church would suit me better."*
—*Winston Churchill*[1]

By now, you might have grown accustomed to the rhythm of this book. We start each chapter with some background information, followed by a conversation that might play out between olim and their parents. We discuss survey data, along with a reality check, and offer some recommendations on how to navigate discussions on each subject matter.

We deviate from this structure here because of the deep emotional nature of the topic. Rather than starting with the ABCs of the IDF or National Service, we start instead with olim's approach to service compared to their Israeli-born counterparts. We follow it with a discussion of the options for olim, rights for lone soldiers compared to those serving in National Service, and close out the chapter with a reality check and suggestions for parents and olim.

On a personal note, this was the most difficult chapter for us to write because the subject matter hits home in more ways than one. We are parents of an Israeli Air Force officer and a soon-to-be soldier, both of whom have risen to overcome their own challenges in Israel. We have also witnessed the trials and tribulations, albeit different ones, faced by so many lone soldiers who have crossed our threshold. Despite our ability to navigate many Israeli systems, we found that we were often powerless to help our own children, let alone others.

The purpose of this chapter is to give olim and their parents a practical approach to understanding what happens during IDF or National Service and the way we see it as both Israeli and American parents. Some challenges olim face during service can be overcome and, in all honesty, some cannot. Our only intention is to manage expectations so that olim and their parents can better understand what is at stake, how to communicate with one another during this trying period, and where to turn for help.

The Emotional Connection-Olim and Israelis

Young adults who decide to move to Israel at or near the mandatory draft age are often motivated by their intense desire to protect and serve a country that they see as the only safe haven for Jews—a country that codified into law the right of any Jew, anywhere, to become a citizen of the modern State of Israel just because of their faith.

The Dialogue

As we noted in Chapter 2, defense of the country can become "*the*" basis for aliya, and the conversation between parents and young olim can sound something like this:

Oleh	Parent
"I always saw it as a responsibility to serve my homeland."	
	"A lovely but dangerous sentiment."
"I have felt this duty ever since our first visit."	
	"You are too young to even understand the solemn nature of army service."

"I fell in love with the land, and I want to protect its people."

"I heard that the IDF doesn't need any more soldiers."

These types of exchanges do not take place in Israeli homes, perhaps because we know the day is coming or simply because we tend not to glorify IDF service.

Every Israeli parent remembers opening the mailbox and finding an IDF draft notice addressed to their 17-year-old who is likely in 11th grade. Whether your child was born in Israel or became an Israeli citizen at a young age, everyone receives their *tzav rishon,* initial commanding orders to appear at the IDF's local recruitment office for a battery of tests that begins a long and winding road to army service that might be as far as two or three years away.

Tzav rishon
Initial IDF draft orders received by a recruit

It was a sobering day when the first commanding orders arrived in our mailbox for our children. Despite the multitude of questions we had about the process, we reluctantly accepted that there was only so much we understood and even less we could do about the process our children embarked on. The same will be the case for parents of olim who join the IDF.

Yom HaZikaron
Israel's Memorial Day honoring those who died in service of the country or in terror attacks

The sense of duty and the danger that accompanies IDF service are perhaps reasons you won't find too many Israeli homes describing it in tones that could be interpreted as glorification. There is nothing glorious about our solemn *Yom HaZikaron,* Memorial Day, when sirens wail for two minutes and everyone, including Israeli kindergarten children, stands at attention, bowing their heads in memory of soldiers who died so they could live.

For a number of years, Israel held military parades on *Yom Ha'Atzmaut* (Independence Day), the day that immediately follows Memorial Day. We haven't had one since 1973. The concept has been raised a few times but has encountered criticism from various corners of society and ultimately the idea was scrapped, perhaps another testament to our desire to recognize IDF service for what it is—a grave duty that ought not be celebrated with military parades.

The IDF is a venerated Israeli institution, and service is something that must be done, a rite of passage that is ingrained, and it is scary. Every Israeli family is separated, at best, by one or two degrees from a family who has endured a tragedy. Soldiers can, and do, die in training accidents. Soldiers can, and do, die in what might seem to be "mini" rounds of conflict that have characterized the past decade. Soldiers can, and do, struggle with the ethical difficulties they can be placed in.[2] Soldiers can, and do, come home with post-traumatic stress disorder. We'd rather live without mandatory service and, simply put, if we didn't have to serve, we wouldn't. It is a grave duty that comes with a price we wish we did not have to pay.

It might be sacrilege to say so, but many Israelis know that army service can be boring. Those in combat units endure months of physical training and, at the end of their training, find themselves sitting for hours and hours on end, staring at a border or guarding a base. It is unfair to say that they are "looking for action," because no one really wants any kind of war. Yet, after months and months of training, many find themselves in jobs that genuinely test the limits of boredom.

Somewhere along the way, no matter what job you have in the army, and regardless of whether you are an oleh or not, soldiers start looking at their *pazam* (פז״מ) app, which tells them how many days they have served alongside a countdown of how many they have left. Somewhere between the end of basic training and the end of service, many soldiers, again regardless of whether they are olim or native Israelis, start to exhibit what is called *sh'vuz* (שבז) behavior. *Sh'vuz* is an acronym for "shover et ha'zayin,"[3] colloquially meaning a soldier is just sick and tired of army service—and tends to show it.

Everyone who serves, regardless of their position, deserves the nation's honor and respect, but do not confuse honor or respect with glorification. Different tones can be detected when young olim talk about joining the IDF vs. their Israeli counterparts. Although olim and their parents can and should be proud that they joined the ranks of native Israelis in defense of the country, approaching this solemn responsibility by extolling its virtues is at odds with the way Israeli society views this grave obligation.

Many will rightfully note that completion of certain IDF training courses is a celebratory event—for example, completion of basic training for combat soldiers, officer's training, pilot courses, or even swearing in ceremonies. Parents attend their children's completion of these courses with a sense of pride. Yet, these are personal accomplishments, not military ones, a recognition of overcoming extreme physical and emotional hardship, and all these events include speeches by high-ranking IDF officials who note, in one way or another, that we serve because we must and not because there is joy in it.

The State classifies lone soldiers into two groups: *muvhakim*, defined mostly as new immigrants without parents in the country, and those without family support, which is defined mostly as Israeli ultra-Orthodox men or women who choose to serve and are shunned by their families. According to a 2018 State Comptroller report, 3,510 (54%) of the 6,150 lone soldiers serving in 2016 were new immigrants (see footnote 8).

To be fair, olim themselves don't understand the IDF road they are about to travel. The same can be said for those who

Sh'vuz
(Shover et hazayin)
Literally breaking one down

P'tor

Waiver from
IDF service

join National Service *(Sherut Leumi),* which is offered as an alternative to those who receive an IDF waiver—a 𝑝'𝑡𝑜𝑟. At any given time, there are about 3,100 to 3,500 young olim who serve in the IDF and roughly 100 olim a year who serve in National Service. All olim arrive with the desire to serve the country but often lack a realistic understanding of what they will confront—and we don't just mean the enemy. We address some of these issues below, including the ease with which olim can enlist without disclosing medical issues.

It bears repeating that the "nuts and bolts" of IDF or National Service are not extensively discussed here. Our goal is to highlight some of the practicalities of service so that olim and their parents are more informed.

Basic Facts on IDF and National Service Tracks

A good starting point for IDF-related logistics is Nefesh B'Nefesh and the IDF website www.Mitgaisim.idf.il, where some of the sections are translated into English. Nefesh B'Nefesh also has information about National Service, but the website Sherut-leumi.co.il is all in Hebrew. Please be aware that IDF rules often change, including the mandatory service age for olim, and therefore all olim should make sure they have the most up-to-date information about IDF requirements. Nefesh B'Nefesh can help olim figure out their mandatory service requirement, if any, but they **must** make sure that they receive a clear answer, in writing via e-mail, about their service requirements. We cannot stress enough the importance of talking to other olim who served. It is likely to be your best barometer of what you will be facing.[4]

Mandatory Service Requirements

Israel's "General Security Law" was passed in 1959 and has been amended a few times over Israel's history. In the simplest terms, it requires the following:

■ Men of mandatory age serve 2.5 years.[5]

■ Women of mandatory age serve 2 years.

■ A waiver from mandatory service can be procured from the IDF, regardless of gender. Generally, waivers are issued to Arabs, ultra-Orthodox men, religious women, those who do not pass the physical exam, and those who claim psychological inability to serve.[6]

■ A waiver from service triggers, under certain circumstances, the right to volunteer.

■ Volunteering for the IDF is not required by law and, contrary to popular belief, National Service *(Sherut Leumi)* is not mandated by law.

Before delving into the details of the IDF, it is important to understand the flow of the recruitment process, the tracks available, where and when waivers are relevant, and when *Sherut Leumi* comes into play. The flow can be seen on the next page.

Notice that everything starts with initial commanding orders. Once you get them, there are really only three options: commence IDF testing, seek a deferral, or request a waiver. You cannot start the testing process without an initial commanding order. You also cannot secure a waiver or seek a deferral without

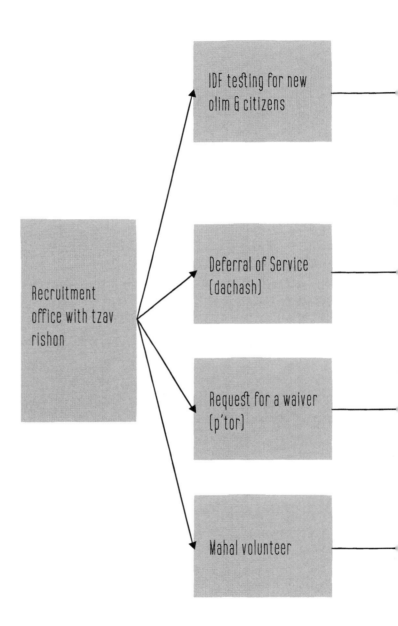

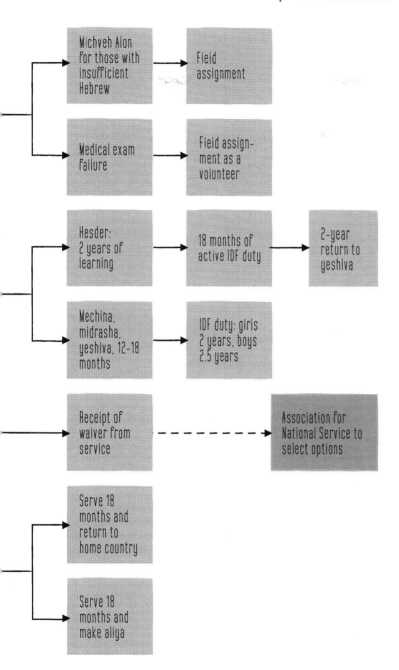

Dachash
(D'chiyat sherut)
Deferral of service

Hesder
IDF-approved program that offers two years of yeshiva learning followed by a maximum of 18 months of IDF active service and ending with another two years of yeshiva learning

Mechina
12- to 18-month gap year program, approved by the Ministry of Defense, that mixes Jewish learning with physical and emotional army preparation

that same piece of paper. Everything starts with the initial commanding orders, and the flow chart demonstrates the tracks available once those have been received. Not all tracks have the same rights; each track is more fully explained below.

Israeli youth, including olim, may secure a *dachash*, deferral of their service, to attend pre-army programs that must be approved by the Ministry of Defense. These can include yeshiva within or outside of the *Hesder* program (described more fully below), *mechina*, *midrasha*, or *shnat sherut* service programs. Most of these programs are in Hebrew; they are culturally "Israeli" and therefore not likely to be beneficial for someone who just recently immigrated.

Women and men alike undergo a series of IDF tests— physical, psychological, personal interviews, and more. The results of these tests, coupled with the IDF's needs at the time, will dictate where a recruit will serve.

To be blunt, this process is not a deeply analytical one. Israeli youth get called for many different types of jobs and undergo many *miyunim* (sorting) processes until they are assigned an army job. Yet, the process is not as thoughtful or as thorough as you might imagine. There is a heavy reliance on tests and short interviews, which don't necessarily translate into a position that best suits a recruit's talents.

Simply put, you go where the IDF puts you, and you might not like where you end up. Olim should understand that the same is true for native Israelis; for this reason alone, they should not be too disappointed with their IDF placement. Perhaps herein lies some of the disenchantment that crops up with olim—the disconnect between expectations of service and the reality.

Mahal-Volunteering for the IDF

An often-overlooked option is volunteering for the IDF without declaring citizenship. *Mahal* units serve 18 months, and the program allows non-Israeli citizens to volunteer in the IDF *without* becoming citizens. At the end of their service, soldiers can return to their home country or start the process of becoming Israeli citizens.

The advantage of *Mahal* is that it gives young people the option to volunteer for the IDF without the burden of Israeli citizenship from the start. A shortened service still affords you the opportunity to learn about the country and the culture without committing to it.

The disadvantages are largely financial. *Mahal* participants don't receive some of the pre-army lone soldier benefits, including housing assistance, language immersion *(ulpan)* or health care. They also receive less housing assistance from certain government offices during their army service, and it can be a reduction that amounts to around NIS 1000. And *Mahal* soldiers who make aliya later on are required to serve in the army for an additional period, depending on their age and family status at the time of aliya.

IDF Testing (Miyunim)

Once 18- to 22-year-old olim become Israeli citizens, their recruitment process begins and they undergo tests, as do all potential recruits. If you think that an adult with many years of evaluation experience decides where a soldier is slotted, think again. The fate of a soldier's placement is at the hands of an 18- or 19-year-old whose job it is to look at the recruits' basic

Midrasha
12- to 24-month gap year program, approved by the Ministry of Defense, that focuses heavily on Jewish texts of all kinds

Shnat sherut
Year of volunteer service in a program approved by the Ministry of Defense

Miyunim
Filtering or sorting process via testing by the IDF to place a recruit in an army position

Mahal
Division of the IDF that allows for noncitizens to volunteer in the IDF for 18 months rather than full required service

information and slot them into an open position, one that needs to be filled immediately. It happens to both Israelis and olim. Not much thought goes into this process, and if recruits are unhappy with their assignments, they should try to fight it and secure additional *miyunim*.

All recruits complete a medical form. We cannot stress enough that recruits should never consider misrepresenting medical facts on their medical forms. There have been a number of press reports on how easy it is for olim to misrepresent or omit their medical history.[7] A recent *Haaretz* article discussed lone soldier suicides, the ease with which lone soldiers can misrepresent their medical histories, and how lone soldiers can easily enlist without proper vetting. The article compares the total number of IDF suicides, which numerically are quite low (15 in each year 2014, 2015, and 2016). In 2018, there was a decrease to 9. Of those suicides, the actual numbers of lone soldiers were 3 (2014), 2 (2015), 1 (2016), 0 (2017), and 2 (2018). The article was written in large part because lone soldier suicides increased to 3 by July 2019.

The *Haaretz* piece reported that young Diaspora Jews account for only 2% of soldiers serving in the Israeli army and that, by most accounts, the vast majority do fine and are a highly motivated group. However, there appears to be a fairly significant vetting problem, with *Haaretz* reporting that, according to the IDF, 14% of foreign-born lone soldiers drop out. There are inadequate background checks, many of the young recruits do not sufficiently comprehend what military life in Israel entails, they see the army as a form of escape from difficulties and challenges they face back home, and they lack the Hebrew needed for absorption. There is evidence of errors of omission and commission on the part of lone soldiers—those who lied about their drug use; did not report that they had emotional problems; claimed they had no medical records when there

were certainly medical issues to be reported; answered "no" to
a series of medical, emotional, and psychiatric questions when
those problems existed; or did not report criminal records.

Misrepresentation of any kind during the IDF vetting
process is dangerous for the recruits, for the men and
women with whom they serve, and for the country. Medical,
emotional, and psychological histories should be disclosed,
and lone soldiers, along with their parents, should try and
understand what motivates their enlistment. As with all aliya
issues, running away from difficulties or challenges in your own
country is likely to be a barrier to successful aliya in general, but
it is even more dangerous during IDF service. Parents should
make every effort to discuss the matter openly with their
children prior to aliya.

There is a misconception that sending children to the army
will "straighten them out." Although it is true that the army is
an unforgettable experience and that it can be extraordinarily
helpful for those needing structure, it is *not* a reformatory
school. No young adult should be sent thousands of miles away
to enlist in an army that fights for our daily existence because
it might "do them good." Parents who think that the IDF is
a good option for their children on this basis ought to think
again. It has the potential to backfire, with dire consequences
for the soldier and the unit.

If the IDF has deemed a recruit medically unfit to serve
(oleh or Israeli-born), that recruit is automatically exempt
from service but can and often does volunteer for service in
units where physical conditioning is not as necessary. Among
Israeli-born youth, those with physical exemptions often end
up serving in computer, telecommunications, intelligence, or
cyber units. Many of these units require high levels of Hebrew
and likely will not be available for olim.

As noted earlier, an immigrant solider without a parent

Chayal boded
A lone soldier without parents in Israel

living in the country is known as a *chayal boded*, and in general, the State categorizes lone soldiers into two groups: "significant," which is defined mostly as new immigrants without parents in the country, and those without family support, which is defined mostly as Israeli ultra-Orthodox men or women who choose to serve and are shunned by their families. The number of lone soldiers who made aliya fluctuates, and there are no concrete numbers.[8] In 2019, Ynet reported that the numbers are unknown; some nonprofit organizations reported the number recently at around 3,150, and the State Comptroller reported the number at 3,510. Lone soldiers who are new immigrants have certain rights unique to them, including a higher salary ostensibly to cover their living expenses, housing allowances, and a full month off once a year to visit parents overseas.

Michveh Alon
Olim soldiers with insufficient Hebrew go to this base to give them intensive language and cultural courses

The IDF evaluates a lone soldier's Hebrew before moving forward with placement. Those who do not pass the language test will be assigned for about two months to *Michveh Alon*, an army base where the IDF offers a wide variety of courses and training in Hebrew language, heritage, and Judaism. A lone soldier's time in *Michveh* gives the army time to better understand the recruit, and only at the end of *Michveh* does the army begin the process of assigning the recruit to an army job, followed by the basic training needed to actually "do" the job.

Those whose Hebrew was found to be sufficient go straight to the sorting and classification process (*miyunim*) until the army decides where to place them. It bears repeating that the fate of a soldier's placement is at the hands of an 18- or 19-year-old whose job it is to look at the recruits' basic information and slot them into an open position. It is not the most thoughtful process in the world; if recruits are unhappy with their assignment, they should push back and try to secure additional *miyunim*.

Hesder Track

The *Hesder* option, an approved IDF deferral track for religious boys, is available to olim and native Israelis alike. Those who select this track are called *beinishim,* bnei yeshiva or boys in yeshiva. The two important factors to know about *Hesder* are that it is a 36- to 48-month program, not including the 17-month army service, and that it is costly to parents.

In general, deferrals are available to all recruits but only if they are registered in a program approved by the Ministry of Defense. Most deferrals are between a year and 18 months, but *Hesder* is unique in that it offers a two-year deferral prior to service, requires only 17 months of service, and allows the recruit to return to yeshiva for another 12 to 25 months. After receipt of initial commanding orders, religious boys complete a deferral of service form effectively indicating that they chose a *Hesder* track.

Hesder allows religious boys to learn Torah in a *Misrad HaBitachon*—Ministry of Defense—approved yeshiva, instead of immediately joining the IDF. Their initial two years are spent in a yeshiva,[9] followed by a shortened IDF service for 17 months and a return to yeshiva for another 18 months to two years. The bookended yeshiva periods are considered *sherut l'lo tashlum (shalat),* service without an IDF salary. For all intents and purposes, *Hesder* students are not released from army service until the end of a five-year track.

Depending on the institution, *Hesder* programs come with tuition fees of around NIS 65,000 or more, spread out over the five-year period. Parents or the lone soldiers make the payments to the yeshiva on a monthly basis for a full five-year program, even during the 17 months of active duty, thus distributing tuition costs over a longer period. The monthly cost is intended

Beinishim
(Bnei yeshiva)
Boys who are in yeshiva and draft for shortened active service of 16 to 18 months

Misrad Ha-Bitachon
Ministry of Defense

Shalat
(Sherut l'lo tashlum)
Service without payment, equivalent to administrative unpaid leave

to cover housing, food, and other expenses.

There is a long history to the *Hesder* program, one which we will not address here. There are also societal tensions behind the *Hesder* program. There are those who believe the program is inconsistent with, or makes a mockery of, IDF service requirements. Society can and often does perceive *Hesder* students as those with a privileged option to learn for four years without sharing equally in the military burden. The issue of *shivyon ba'netel* (equal burden) is a highly volatile socio-political issue, and the *Hesder* program is not exempt from these debates.

Shivyon ba'netel
Equaliza-tion of socie-tal burdens

Setting aside the societal debates, it is important to note that *Hesder* costs are high, at least for Israelis and perhaps to parents of olim. Lone soldiers who join the *Hesder* program and their parents should be aware of the time commitment and the costs, for these costs are separate from what comes after, like university. Lone soldiers who believe that the IDF's salary and monetary benefits will cover all of the *Hesder* expenses are misguided. Even if lone soldiers earned enough during their service to pay a large portion of *Hesder* costs, they will be left with no cushion when their *Hesder* program is over. And by the time that *Hesder* ends, lone soldiers are no longer qualified to receive benefits from immigration services.

To those who think that *Hesder* participants can defray their *Hesder* costs by working during their summers or holidays, think again. As we indicated earlier, the first two years and the last two years of *Hesder* are considered unpaid administrative leave. Anyone in this status is legally prohibited to work in Israel.

Responsibility to Lone Soldiers

Mashakit Tash
Army office responsible for the conditions of service

As indicated, in any one year, there are between 3,100 and 3,500 lone soldiers whose origins are from outside Israel. The IDF assigns special personnel (a *Mashakit Tash*) to make sure that lone soldiers receive everything they are entitled to although, more often than not, lone soldiers will have to continue to pester that individual to ensure that all rights are afforded.

The constant badgering of a *Mashakit* can be draining on soldiers because they barely succeed in keeping their heads above water. They don't have the time for constant messages, they often don't have cell service when they are on duty, and their Hebrew skills are an obstacle to getting what they need— particularly since a *Mashakit* will make every effort to push lone soldiers' Hebrew to the limit in the name of trying improving their language skills.

Frankly, it is wise to get used to the "badgering" process because it is simply part of Israeli life and it will come up again and again in every aspect of Israeli systems, from education to health care. In other words, don't give up on the *Mashakit* and get used to pestering people because it is how things get done in Israel.

Many have heard of the FIDF (Friends of the IDF), a nonprofit that raises funds for all IDF soldiers, and while it certainly assists lone soldiers, its cause is a far wider one: FIDF's fundraising supports all IDF soldiers and not just lone soldiers. Lone soldier nonprofit organizations have come and gone over the years. Those that are still around really do exist to help lone soldiers during and after their service while offering information to parents as well. As of this writing, the Lone Soldier Center in Memory of Michael Levin, the Michael Levin Base, Keep Olim, and Nefesh B'Nefesh are among the more widely known organizations with a variety of programs for lone soldiers and their parents. There is a Nefesh B'Nefesh/ FIDF 24/7 hotline to support lone soldiers and their families in need or in crisis. There is also a new Nefesh B'Nefesh program designed especially for North American parents of lone soldiers. The program includes video conferences with commanding officers, monthly newsletters, and subsidized flights to attend IDF ceremonies for those who cannot afford to fly in for one.

For all intents and purposes, the IDF is more like an "at home" army in the sense that soldiers come home for the weekend, sometimes infrequently, but they do return home. They bring their laundry home, and it is often full of heavy and smelly army uniforms. It isn't unusual for parents to drive to a base and bring soldiers home-cooked meals to give them a boost when they are on base for 21 days in a row or when they had a particularly hard week. Being an "at home" army means that native-born soldiers with parents in the country have a home to go back to, parents who help with laundry and food and general well-being. Soldiers who come to Israel without family miss "home" quite a bit, even if they say they can manage without it.

Our experience tells us that families who "adopt" lone soldiers can be of great assistance to them and to National Service volunteers. Adoption does not necessarily mean living in a family home. Some organizations claim that lone soldiers and National Service participants do not want to live with a family on a regular basis and that they prefer having their own apartments to come home to. Even if they live on their own, adoption can mean hosting for holidays or weekends; taking care of them when they are sick; helping them through bureaucracy; and, most importantly, becoming a "go-to" resource for them. There isn't a formal way to become a *mishpacha m'ametzet*, a family

Mishpacha m'ametzet
Adoptive family for lone soldiers or National Service participants

that adopts lone soldiers or National Service participants. These relationships tend to happen by word of mouth. See Chapter 6, "Friends and Family, and Friends Who Become Family," for the relationship between adopted families and olim.

National Service

As noted earlier in this chapter, waivers or exemptions from IDF service can be claimed only *after* you have received initial draft orders. In other words, every child at the age of 17 (give or take) and those who arrive between the ages of 17 and 22 receive their draft orders, regardless of gender.

Ultra-Orthodox men and religious women receive the very same orders as everyone else, as do Arab men and women who are Israeli citizens. You must appear at the local recruitment office *(Lishkat HaGiyus)* to ask for an exemption.[10] In the case of ultra-Orthodox men and religious women, after a relatively perfunctory check by the IDF, requests for religious waivers are generally honored. A waiver also means that these individuals do not undergo any battery of IDF tests since they have their waiver in hand.

Any man or woman receiving an IDF waiver is completely excused from service and need not serve in the IDF at all. Nor are they required to serve in National Service. However, once their waiver is recorded in the IDF system, they are offered the option of National Service. Those who choose National Service take the paperwork to the Association for National Service, which is *not* part of the IDF. Again, National Service *is not* required by law, but it is the path taken by Israeli religious women, although men can register as well.

National Service options cannot be exercised until an exemption from the IDF is received. If you don't have that

Lishkat HaGiyus
IDF recruitment office. No one is allowed in there other than recruits or soldiers— no parents, siblings, or friends allowed

exemption signed by the IDF, the National Service system will not even consider any service options for you. The Association for National Service has volunteer options available on its website, but much of them are in Hebrew.

Options for National Service vary from working in a hospital to working in an old age home, working with the challenged or disabled population, or working in a kindergarten. The quality of your Hebrew impacts the options available, and nearly all of the jobs are posted in Hebrew. As of this writing, there is one organization, Here Next Year, which currently posts National Service jobs in English. Service can be one or two years, although written contracts are uncommon, which leaves both sides unprotected.

Yom siddurim
Extra days off for lone soldiers to run errands

Benefits for olim performing National Service differ from those given to lone soldiers under the IDF system. They don't receive a housing allowance or *yom siddurim,* errand days to take care of their personal matters. Regarding housing, the government places all National Service participants in apartments, yet olim don't have homes to go back to on the weekends, leaving them to fend for themselves. National Service participants also have no built-in system to voice complaints, concerns, or challenges, whereas lone soldiers at least have a *Mashakit Tash* within the IDF. Finally, adoption of lone soldiers is a far more acceptable and known concept, but that is not the case for National Service volunteers, who are just as much in need. As with lone soldiers, there is no formal system to adopt those in National Service, but they would benefit greatly from a relationship with families who become a resource for them, just as any lone soldier would.

Remember the IDF's *Mahal* program we noted earlier where a noncitizen can volunteer for the IDF for 18 months without having to make aliya? Such an option is *not* available to anyone in National Service. In other words, National

Service is only available to citizens. For all intents and purposes, this means that olim who prefer National Service must first become citizens, receive their draft orders, and *only then* receive their exemption signed by the IDF before they are "moved over" to the National Service system. This process can take a few months and, in the meantime, olim are left without any housing or other structure of support until their National Service job kicks in.

Why does it take so long for olim to receive a religious waiver? The reason for the delay is relatively simple. The IDF's recruitment office knows how to check the validity of Israeli citizens' religious waiver requests by looking up their identity number and the school system they were registered in and through a cursory view of the requestor's digital footprint for telltale signs that they are not as religious as they claim. There is some work involved for the IDF before consenting to a religious waiver, but the IDF knows what it is looking for, and it is a fairly quick process to receive an exemption for this purpose.

Contrast this with olim who show up to a recruitment office claiming a religious exemption without any history in Israel. The IDF has a hard time ascertaining their religious status for the most part because of a lack of understanding of the school system overseas. Jewish day schools outside of Israel are foreign entities to IDF staff; conversely, there are religious students who attend public schools overseas, a complete anomaly to the IDF. As a result, olim seeking an exemption so that they can be moved to the National Service system will likely wait until the IDF confirms their status, and it can take time.

Public Perception of Lone Soldiers vs. National Service Participants

As we noted in Chapter 1, service to the country carries a very high value and along with it a positive public perception. The same cannot be said for National Service. There is very little data on the public perception of National Service or even a participant's view of the service. One study showed that most are motivated by their will to serve the country. An overwhelming majority are satisfied with their service experience, and a considerable group felt that National Service significantly benefits society.[11] Another study similarly found that altruism overwhelmingly motivates National Service, there was overall satisfaction with their service, and a high majority (87%) felt satisfied with the level of public appreciation of their service.[12] However, despite positive attitudes toward the work, a majority of respondents complained about service conditions such as low salaries, and 20% of those who indicated that they were satisfied with the public's appreciation also indicated that people do not think of them as being part of Israeli society because they have not served in the IDF:

> Respondents stressed the bitterness that they felt about inadequate recognition from the public or the referral organization (Eisenberg, 2000), a feeling shared by volunteers studied elsewhere (e.g., Stevens, 1991). That the public is unaware of the fact that National Service volunteers do important work and that they are treated like any other worker is a key problem in this study, a finding supported by others as well (e.g., Handy et al., 2000).[13]

This public perception problem is one that continues to plague those who volunteer in National Service. It can be seen in the treatment that National Service olim receive. For instance, on their aliya flight, they do not receive special T-shirts noting that that they are making aliya straight to service, unlike lone soldiers who are heralded even on their aliya flight. Across the board, National Service has no uniforms, making those serving hard to identify. On some level, so long as National Service volunteers "look" different from the IDF, they will always be seen as substituting a social duty for IDF enlistment. Public perception is an important issue for National Service volunteers to internalize before they arrive in Israel.

Health Care and Injuries During Service

For all intents and purposes, soldiers are considered "property" of the IDF; therefore, all health care needed, either on an emergency basis or as a matter of course, is under the auspices of IDF doctors, the quality of which is addressed more fully below. National Service volunteers remain under the general public health care system available to every citizen. The pros and cons of socialized medicine in Israel are beyond the scope of this book, although olim and their parents should bone up on the system and how to work within it.

Much is left to be desired when it comes to IDF health care. One good thing about a centralized and mandatory draft is that the IDF, on occasion, detects health conditions that draftees might not know they had or a vaccine that needs a booster. Most bases have a clinic staffed with primary care physicians who can handle relatively basic care, from a flu shot to dehydration, and perhaps a fairly standard bone break. The army has excellent trauma-related care, in the sense that there are whole units of medics and paramedics who become experts in dealing with battlefield injuries. But otherwise, the army is not staffed with specialists, like an orthopedic surgeon or a neurologist, should you need it.

Unfortunately, we know what happens when you do need a specialist, and sometimes the care is adequate enough to be satisfactory. A soldier who needs to see a specialist receives a referral from an army doctor and then can make an appointment to be seen by the appropriate doctor within the public health system. The same can be said for diagnostic testing. If you need an MRI, for instance, a soldier can get a referral and will be sent to a facility within the public health system that is reimbursed by the IDF. As indicated, run-of-the-mill tests and even MRIs are available, albeit slow, and you can largely be satisfied with what you might consider "standard" tests or care.

Complications arise when the injury is more severe, and often the army is late in acknowledging that the injury is a serious one that needs immediate care. This is where adoptive parents become *in loco parentis* and advocate for a young soldier who hardly wants to admit to an injury.

It is crucial to understand, and always remember, that a social contract exists between the IDF and parents of IDF soldiers. We lend you our children, and the IDF is responsible for returning them whole—physically and mentally. Many perceive this social contract as one that applies only during combat. This is simply not the case. Once soldiers are on an army base of any kind or are otherwise in transit for any purpose during service, the IDF is responsible for them. Period. In practical terms, this means that when soldiers fall down on base or miss a step purely by accident, having nothing to do with any military exercise, the IDF is responsible for their care today, tomorrow, and well into the future. It means that soldiers not only have a right to fully paid medical care by the army but also are entitled to certain percentages of handicapped status *(achuz neichut)*, which carries with it a host of rights.

A handicapped soldier might not have an injury you can see. It can be on the post-traumatic stress spectrum that came simply from a standard or a perceived uneventful service, or it can be a broken hip that came simply from missing a step on base.

Unfortunately, we recall these incidences because we experienced them first-hand. On what was a normal Saturday night, our first lone soldier simply missed a step while walking on base. It took a few hours until he was seen by an army doctor and ultimately was sent to Soroka Hospital in Beer Sheva, where, despite our involvement, he languished for a few days until he underwent surgery. Pins were placed in his hip, but the wait caused him necrosis and permanent hip damage, something that took about two years to discover and fix.

It was clear very early on that our lone soldier was not returning to army service after his injury. For injured soldiers, there is a purgatory-like status that sits between active duty and discharged due to injury. That status is called *ram shtayim*, (Ram 2) when an injured soldier is referred by an army doctor to a hospital through an official form.

Because there are no designated army hospitals in Israel, all soldiers are admitted and treated in public hospitals, paid for by the army. Even when released from the hospital, injured soldiers remain in Ram 2 status until doctors decide whether they can return to active duty. Rehabilitative care facilities are also within the Ram 2 system. As of this writing, there are Ram 2 offices with telephone numbers in the Jerusalem, Tel Aviv, North, Sharon, and Shefayla regions. Every hospital also has a telephone number that is associated with a Ram 2 official and, from an administrative standpoint, it is important to know that Ram 2 personnel are other soldiers and not hospital representatives. Absent a full release from the army, anyone in

Achuz neichut
Percentage of handicap— i.e., what percentage of the body isn't functioning

Ram shtayim
(r'shima m'kuvetzet) A grouped list that really doesn't explain why this unit has this name. It is colloquially known as Ram 2

Ram 2 status is not an active soldier or a civilian and generally cannot leave the country while in this Ram 2 status.

If you don't know how to maneuver within the Ram 2 stage, you can easily (as did we) get frustrated trying to fill prescriptions at regular pharmacies or trying to speak to doctors who will likely only communicate directly with soldiers.

Our lone soldier rehabilitated at our home for a few months after pins were placed in his hip. It was clear that his discharge was only a matter of time, and his rehabilitative months were used to consider next steps, including university studies. Because the injury did not happen in combat or during a training exercise, our lone soldier was exceedingly hesitant to undergo evaluation for handicapped status. Admirably, he felt that seeking such status took advantage of a system that was intended for more "seriously" injured soldiers or ones injured in combat or during military exercises.

With the help of his parents overseas, we reiterated the social contract between the IDF and parents. We lend you our children for defense of the country and you give them back whole. It does not matter how a soldier was injured. It is enough that the injury took place on army property. We also explained the need to contemporaneously document the injury, within the Ministry of Defense system, from the beginning of the injury through surgery, multiple post-surgery visits to the orthopedist, and the recommendation to ultimately undergo a hip replacement at the age of 24. Although we maintained a record of every doctor's meeting and every piece of medical paper issued, there is significance in maintaining contemporaneous records, for no one can guarantee that the Ministry of Defense would agree to foot any bill issued years after the injury.

Ultimately, our lone soldier requested review for handicap status early on. This meant filing the paperwork and undergoing committee review without us or an attorney present. We saw him through the process and today, while he looks like a perfectly normal 27-year-old, he is registered as having 35% handicapped status. This status will likely entitle him to a handicapped sticker for his car as he ages, some tax credits, and some financial benefits when he seeks a mortgage. These benefits might not seem like much, but failure to document the injury as early as possible would likely make it difficult to seek handicap status post facto.

We maintained contact with our lone soldier's parents throughout the process, sending them the semi-annual updates from medical visits. Again, this is where an adoptive family can help ease the minds of parents who are so far away.

A word about mental health, an issue that lacks awareness among the general population, let alone the IDF. The IDF has improved when it comes to acknowledging the need for mental health professionals and has a specific position designated for it known as a *kaban*. If soldiers have a concern, they can seek out a *kaban* for assistance. Often soldiers eschew going to a *kaban* for fear it will taint their army record in some way. We indicated previously that a soldier's health care is the sole responsibility of the IDF, and while that certainly is the case for mental health, this is an area where paying for outside help could be warranted. A psychologist who speaks English might be worth every penny for a soldier who is suffering, and parents would be wise to consider financing this cost if they feel it is necessary.

Parents of IDF soldiers pray that the soldiers are as healthy coming out of service as they were going in. We also know that there is no guarantee. There is, however, an unspoken agreement between parents and the IDF. Return them to us as they were, and if that isn't possible, the IDF and the Ministry of Defense must take responsibility. There is nothing to be ashamed of in

Kaban
(katzin l'briyut nefesh)
Mental health officer

ensuring that soldiers' rights, and the rights of their families, are exercised to the fullest extent of the law. The social contract between parents and the IDF must be honored.

Now that we have identified some of the tracks available for olim and some of the pros and cons of each, here are some statistics of what IDF or National Service olim had to say.

Among our survey respondents who served in Israel, 71% served in the IDF and 29% did National Service. We asked parents and olim a wide variety of questions about IDF and National Service, including whether they felt they had sufficient information about service options, whether olim had sufficient care during their service, and whether their feelings about service changed after completion.

Regarding service options, respondents were asked whether there was sufficient information available about their options prior to their service (Figure 1).

Figure 1: Prior to IDF or National Service, you had sufficient information about the service options available

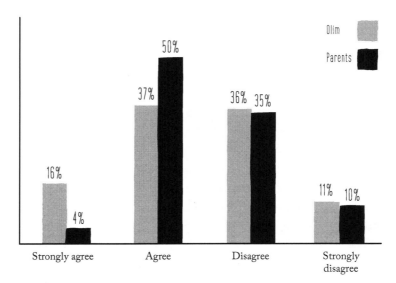

Nearly half of parents (45%) and olim (47%) disagree that they had sufficient information prior to service, and it is troubling to see that both sides, in almost equal measure, believe they lacked enough information before drafting.

When asked whether the olim received appropriate care during their service, nearly a third of olim indicated that they did not (Figure 2).

Figure 2: During IDF of National Service, olim received appropriate care

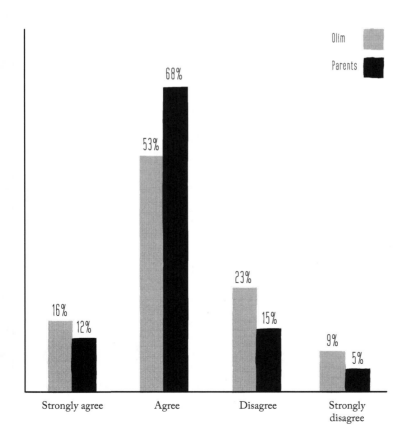

Although a high percentage of olim (69%) agreed or strongly agreed that they received appropriate care, parents believed it even more (80%). A troubling data point is the 32% of olim who do not believe that they received appropriate care during their service—only 20% of parents believe that care was lacking. When looking at this data as a whole, we believe that parents have a high regard of the care offered their children during their service because they are largely not here to evaluate it on their own.

Finally, we looked at post-service to see whether there was a change in attitude toward service after completion (Figure 3).

The data in Figure 3 shows that 63% of olim agree or strongly agree that they felt differently about service after completion, compared to 52% of parents. We did not ask whether the change in attitude was positive or negative.

Figure 3: I felt differently about the IDF of National Service after completion

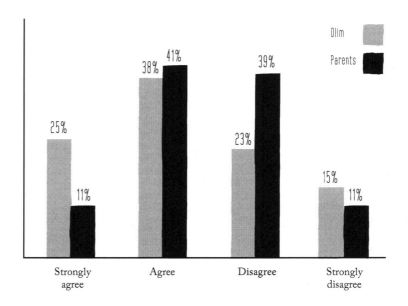

⊘ Reality Check

The reality regarding Israel's mandatory draft is that nearly everyone who serves, olim and native born, wants a meaningful service. And who wouldn't? If you are already committed to taking two to three years out of your life to serve, it might as well be consequential. And herein lies part of the disillusionment with army service. Regardless of whether you are an oleh or a native, you might not get the IDF job you want and you might not get the job that most suits your talents. And even if you are assigned the very job you want, be prepared for it to raise all sorts of morally complicated issues you never thought of before. Be prepared for it, or National Service, to be boring. Be prepared for rules that really make very little sense. Below are our top list of "truths" that come with IDF or National Service to keep in mind:

■ **Mandatory service means you go where they put you:** It is applicable to olim and to the native born. You might not be saving the country, or even anyone in particular, but like any other solider, you will be a cog in a very large machine. A lack of Hebrew skills can indeed translate into a less-desirable post, and while the country on the whole values IDF service, you might not feel the love when you are trying to just make it through the day. Please know that you are often faced with moral dilemmas that you never expected.

■ **Don't confuse success with efficiency:** The IDF is recognized worldwide for its military achievements and its innovation. Yet, it is a behemoth of an organization, and from the outside (a parent's perspective), there seems to be little order and a lot of last-minute changes that deeply affect soldiers' lives and the lives of their families. It will look like a large, dysfunctional, disorganized, and impersonal institution, and efficiency is not its middle name.

■ **Don't equate army with excitement:** Your service, even if you are in combat, can be boring. Your National Service might not be as exciting as it claims to be. Be prepared for whatever it is to be different than what you thought it would be. Please try to avoid comments like "it's not fair." Life isn't fair, and this might be as good a time as any to learn that lesson.

■ **Be truthful:** It is dangerous to lie, misrepresent, or omit anything about your medical, emotional, or psychiatric history. If you are running away from challenges, think again about IDF service. Never count on the IDF to vet olim for any of these issues. The manpower isn't there, and olim lack the long vetting road that most Israelis start in 11th grade.

M'fakdim
Command-ing officers

■ **It is not summer camp or a reformatory school:** Camp counselors build campers' self-esteem and an overall positive environment. *M'fakdim,* commanding officers in the army, can build morale, but they also can make you weary and erode your enthusiasm. They have a job to do, and it is not to ensure soldiers' happiness. Commanding officers know when they have a lone soldier in their ranks but they can occasionally forget that, unlike other soldiers, lone soldiers spend nearly all of their free time running errands, doing laundry, and cooking—all of which would otherwise be taken care of by Israeli families.

■ **You can lose sight of the forest:** Lone soldiers who came to save the nation will find themselves trying to just make it through the day. If you are a proverbial cog in the IDF wheel, it will be hard to see your impact (the forest) because you can barely see the tree.

- **Going in healthy and coming home healthy:** There is a social contract between the IDF and parents. We give them our children and they return them healthy in body, mind, and spirit. The IDF is responsible for an injured soldier, whether it is a minor or major injury. Fight for those rights. And where mental health is concerned, if needed, consider paying for counseling outside the army system for a soldier who needs it.

- **The end of the road:** Don't be surprised if a soldier or National Service volunteer starts counting down the days until service ends. Despite a gung-ho attitude at the beginning of army or National Service, you are not the only one who will be itching for it to end. Native Israelis do too.

- **National Service:** You must make aliya to volunteer for National Service, and the process will take time. Don't expect to land and immediately start your service, which means you must have a plan of where and how to live for a temporary period. There isn't a formalized or organized system like the IDF that sorts you for assignments, and much of it will be up to you. Regretfully, National Service does not receive the same venerated position as IDF service, and this is the case even with Israelis.

- **Shorthand:** The IDF runs the army on shorthand. If there is a word that can be made into a three-letter abbreviation, the IDF will do it. In fact, most of the words are entirely abbreviations. IDF soldiers throw words around that no one in the general population uses. They will explain the shorthand once, and they won't have patience to explain it again. In Appendix B, you will find abbreviations that took us years to learn, and they are not the only ones. Try to keep up to date, or just be prepared not to ask any questions, letting the lone soldier drone on without you understanding it. We do it all the time, and we are no longer embarrassed by our lack of knowledge.

Tag
Shoulder tag that identifies your base or unit

Sika
A pin that identifies the type of job you have

Masa kumta
Long journey carrying quite a bit of heavy gear to receive your beret

Tekes hash'ba'a
Swearing in ceremony

■ **Ceremonies:** More than most, combat soldiers have a number of bite-sized accomplishments that come with official ceremonies. Among them are receiving a *tag* for the brigade; a *sika* for the unit; the *masa kumta;* and the *tekes hash'ba'a.* We understand that it is difficult and costly to travel to Israel, and no one expects parents to come to all these events. Yet, it is worthwhile to decide which one parents can attend. And if parents cannot be present, it will be very meaningful to have other family members, friends, or an adoptive family present. It is always nice to know that someone is there for lone soldiers when they pass these IDF milestones. Know that the ceremony dates are always subject to change, so if you bought a ticket to accommodate that date, you might need to change it. At certain ceremonies, it is expected that parents, biological or adopted, bring food—a lot of it. Don't be embarrassed when certain families lay out a spread that you can't compete with. Native Israeli mothers are better at this, hands down. Alas, there are no similar ceremonies for those who are in National Service.

■ **Getting to know "them":** In a perfect world, parents should know the identity and telephone number of their children's commanding officer. Arguably, language barriers might complicate the communication, but knowing this information is crucial for both the lone soldiers and the parents. Although it would be ideal to know the identity of a similarly responsible individual in the case of National Service, the ambiguous nature of the system probably makes it harder to identify the one person who is responsible for such a volunteer, although we have done it and believe that it helps ensure that certain responsibilities are met.

■ **The post-army trip (it's inevitable):** All Israelis serving in the IDF need to decompress from the pressures of the military, and many do so by traveling abroad. Some do so for a month or two, and others do it for as much as a year. Don't be surprised if they want to travel to distant places to get away from it all. It's normal. Every Israeli does it. We don't love it either, but, as they say in Hebrew, "zeh ma sh'yesh," this is what it is.

☐ Reframing the Mandatory Service Period

As we have done in prior chapters, we outline below what olim and parents should keep in mind as they both pass through the IDF or National Service. Our suggestions are based on our experiences, and we have reason to believe that young adults might discount our suggestions but, at the absolute minimum, we hope that both parents and olim will be well served by our guidance below.

Olim: Serving in the IDF is dangerous, and while Israel appreciates every soldier who serves, we don't glorify it and you shouldn't either. Whether you serve in the IDF or National Service, do not lie about your medical condition, for it helps no one and it is arguably dangerous. It also can be boring, so please don't be surprised by the fact that your day to day might not have as much action as you anticipated. "Organized" is not the word you should associate with either the IDF or National Service; get used to standing up for yourself, because it will stand you in good stead. If you choose *Hesder*, remember that it is costly. If you choose National Service, remember that it takes time for your processing and that your conditions will appear less than your lone soldier friends. There are negative effects of IDF service. The same can be said for those in National Service who are exposed to very saddening conditions. Please reach out to anyone you can to get help.

Apropos of reaching out, find an adoptive family somehow. Post on Facebook, reach out to friends, or find a friend of a friend who can help. You might not be living with an adoptive family, but such a family can be of invaluable assistance to you when you really need it. This family can be your safe space, a place where you can complain and no one will judge you for it. Most importantly, an adoptive family does not make you weak. It makes you resourceful.

Parents: Even Israeli parents find the system maddening, and they often can do little to help their own children. Being thousands of miles away from a conflict zone renders you even more impotent. The IDF is a "home" army in the sense that coming home for food, sleep, and basic comforts makes a real difference in the life of soldiers. You can't help them on the weekends, offer a home-cooked meal, do their laundry, or logistically handle any issue that is needed. If you know someone in Israel who can help, draft them into service on behalf of your child.

A few words of wisdom and pitfalls to avoid. Your children will definitely complain about the system; they will be weary, annoyed, and will often not see the point of their service. Do not mock their decision to serve, throw their decision back in their face, or say "I told you so." This is how it is for everyone, even the native born. You will not understand why your children don't get enough sleep, why you don't hear from them as often, and why their abbreviated Hebrew doesn't resemble words you thought you knew. Know when their ceremonies are, try to be there for them even if they don't ask, or ask someone to represent you. Know their commanding officer's identity and telephone number, because it will bring you peace of mind. Do everything in your power to ensure that your children accurately represent themselves during the IDF vetting process. Be conscious of their mental state, and if you aren't sure, reach out to someone who knows them well enough to keep you in the loop. And it bears repeating: if you can, find a family who can adopt them, because those people will be your "lifeline" to your child.

🗨 Constructive Dialogue

Olim
"I am tired, I don't understand anything, and
I hate this."

Parents
"It must be really hard. We are with you
every step of the way."

8

University

"So how do you know what is the right path to choose to get the result that you desire? The honest answer is this: You won't."

—Jon Stewart, Comedian, Commencement Speech 2004, College of William and Mary[1]

According to the OECD, Israelis are among the oldest university[2] students in the world and, according to Israel's Council on Higher Education, Israeli students begin their higher-education studies on average six years later than their peers abroad.[3] Recent OECD data shows that, in Israel, 70% of young people leave education between the ages of 18 and 24— in other words, they are not enrolled in university because they are either in the army, traveling post-army, engaged in activities including volunteering, or taking the university entrance exam.[4] Overall, the data shows that the median age for receiving a bachelor's degree is 27, far older than their international peers.

To complicate matters, Israeli universities do not offer the same kind of liberal arts education as their North American counterparts, and there are very few multidisciplinary tracks; the system is most comparable to European universities. Applicants are required to declare a major (also known as a *chug*), a course of study, before they set foot in a classroom. In fact, in many cases, they are required to be accepted by a department before they are accepted to the university. Israeli students typically take the psychometric college entrance exam, but the SATs are also increasingly accepted at certain schools. Although students can change their minds and select a different major, most try to make up their minds and stick with one to avoid wasting even more time and delaying their graduation. Most Israeli students work part time to cover part of their tuition or rent or to subsidize simple quality-of-life events.

Chug
In this context, a course of study (i.e., law)

For the most part, tuition is far cheaper than it is in other countries. Tuition at public universities is about NIS 14,000 per year, and at private universities it is around NIS 60,000 per year, a fraction of tuition at similar schools in the United States. Some olim will have their tuition completely covered, and most will have a deep discount; either way, most Israeli college students work part time in addition to their studies to fund leisure activities, food, rent, and more. Please note that olim may need to pay the tuition and subsequently be reimbursed for it. See the Nefesh B'Nefesh website for a better understanding of the issues surrounding university and to gain access to a consultant who can help with navigating the system.

The deadline for application to university can be a moving target and can vary from university to university and even from department to department within the same university. University students all over the world often find themselves in a fairly long application process, but that is not necessarily the case in Israel. University starts *after* the Jewish holidays, which can mean that acceptance to a program comes as late as September and at the last minute. In some cases, an applicant can be accepted a week before the academic year starts. The application process and internal departmental exams or interviews are very specific, and it is important to track the requirements and the deadlines, for they differ widely. An important gatekeeper in the process is often the secretary in the department, who can offer invaluable information about your requirements, deadlines, paperwork, and other issues related to the acceptance process.

As we noted in Chapter 1, a degree from an Israeli university eases absorption, but don't ignore the high level of language skills required to enroll. Those who completed the army or National Service will have greater language capability but perhaps not enough for certain university programs. There are certain Hebrew-language tests, like the *Mivchan Yael,* a Hebrew proficiency exam, that might be required before olim can be matriculated. Some universities allow olim to take Hebrew courses at university in lieu of the Yael exam or if a sufficient score was not secured.

While most olim will be allowed to submit exams or papers

Mivchan Yael
Timed Hebrew proficiency exam

in English, this is not a hard and fast rule, and don't assume that this leniency will make learning easier. Pre-academic programs known as *mechina,* are also available, required in some cases, which might give olim more time to consider a course of study. Some colleges or universities offer English-only programs or tracks, but tuition is more expensive. Nevertheless, those with language challenges should consider this option.

If olim explore colleges in Israel, there are a few English-speaking ones—for example, the Inter-Disciplinary Center (IDC),[5] Hebrew University's Rothberg School,[6] and Bar Ilan University[7]— with both undergraduate and graduate programs for international students. All of these institutions offer English-only degree-granting programs, but they are few and far between. Simply put, Hebrew is a necessity at any college in Israel—period.

There are dormitory buildings available for students, but some universities or colleges have rules about who can reside in them. Normally, dorms are reserved for students whose families live far away from the campus—i.e., in another city. Perhaps because of their age, most university students prefer to rent apartments together with other students rather than live in the dormitory. Most college students work while they are in school and tend to come to the campus for classes, research, or studying but don't stay there for long. The lack of large dormitories, coupled with working students, makes campus life different than in other countries. Although there are strong student unions, cultural events, and groups that get together formally or informally, student life on campus is less than a vibrant "campus-y" environment. Ben Gurion University (BGU) in Beer Sheva is one of the universities in Israel that worked hard at building an energetic student life on campus. In fact, there is data to suggest that students will often elect to attend BGU over higher-ranked universities like Hebrew

Mechina
Preparatory program before university

University because of BGU's student community.

Finally, there are those who seek to immigrate after they have completed their bachelor's or master's degrees, usually between the ages of 22 and 28, only to find that in certain fields their degrees require certification by government ministries and that they might still need to attend language training for their specific profession. If you have certain licenses that allowed you to practice your profession in your home country, those will require certification by the Ministry of Education. Be prepared to bring your diploma and your official and original transcript. We know of professionals with doctorates who were asked to re-defend their thesis. Even if your profession did not require specific licensure, it is wise to have your undergraduate, graduate, or doctoral degrees certified by the Ministry of Education. All public sector positions ask for this certification, and your diploma from your home country will not be enough. Accordingly, bring your diploma and your transcripts so that the Ministry of Education can officially recognize your degree. Attending specific language immersion training *(ulpan)* for certain professions, like medical doctors, might be necessary to learn Hebrew terminology. Remember that your academic degrees from high-ranking institutions might not impress Israelis, and there is little you can do to change their attitude.

Three-quarters of olim (75%) who responded to our survey indicated that they did not have a university degree before making aliya, yet parents didn't seem to be too concerned about it. As noted in Figure 1, only 31% believed that college was not part of their child's post-aliya plan.

Figure 1: I/parents were concerned that attending college/university was not part of a post-aliya plan

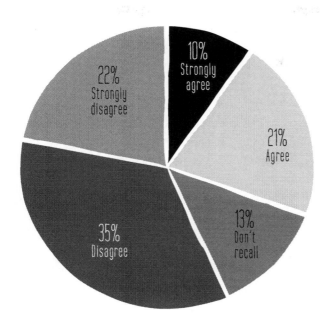

Most young olim will not attend university immediately after making aliya unless they attend one of the English-only programs. In all likelihood, those who made aliya between the ages of 18 and 22 serve in the IDF, or in National Service, and only begin to look at university options in their early or sometimes mid-20s, like many native Israelis.

⊘ Reality Check

The reality is that those who complete IDF or National Service will have a linguistic leg up from other olim, and they might find absorption onto a college campus somewhat easier because of shared life experiences with other Israelis. It does not, however, guarantee smooth sailing to graduation. Don't underestimate how hard it is. Those with the intention of making aliya "straight" to a bachelor's program will find it nearly impossible. English programs are available, but they are limited and much more expensive,[8] and attending them often means you will have kicked the cultural absorption can down the road.[9] Declaring a major right away is not easy, and the university's published requirements for acceptance can change without warning. It is important to consult with others; speak with departmental advisors; and, if need be, ensure that issues are committed to writing.

Olim who have been in Israel for a while and have made it through the IDF, National Service, or short-term employment are strengthened by the fact they have made it this far. They see university as an extension of their success. Parents who failed to convince their children that an education comes *before* immigration will undoubtedly remember that their children promised to secure a degree in Israel.

It is important to reiterate what we said in Chapter 1. The time-honored Jewish social fabric of "my son/daughter the doctor/lawyer" is not applicable in Israel. Doctors and lawyers can earn less than entrepreneurs. Salaries in Israel often work differently, and unquestionably doctors and lawyers in Israel will earn less than they would overseas, but other occupations in the tech world are in very high demand and very well-paid. Just as degrees from the best educational institutions don't translate in Israel, the same goes for careers that come after education. Young olim who are determined to stay in Israel will choose educational paths or even educational institutions that might not impress parents but have a better chance of resulting in a decent-paying job.

☐ Reframing the University Era

The pros and cons surrounding an Israeli college education, for both olim and their parents, should be guided by the following:

🕊 **Olim**: Even if you served in the IDF or National Service, you will be expected to have a high level of Hebrew before you are accepted to Israeli universities. Don't be insulted if Israeli universities require you to enroll in a pre-academic *mechina* to improve your language skills. Don't be surprised if learning in Hebrew is harder than you expected. Among education professionals, it is well-accepted that language acquisition and proficiency occur through college. Don't be afraid to change your major if it does not suit you. Don't be disappointed in yourself if you are considering English programs. Don't hesitate to talk to other students before enrolling so you better understand student life and the courses you will be taking. Don't be afraid to choose something that you might have completely rejected in your country of birth. A career path here is different than where you came from, and it is more than reasonable to decide on a course of study you might have otherwise shied away from.

🐚 **Parents:** If you were educated outside of Israel, university life in Israel will be far from your own experiences. Your children are older than you were when you started university. Choose to see it as a good thing, because they are more mature and perhaps their decisions on courses of study are more grounded than they otherwise would have been. The acceptance process and the road to graduation will be difficult. Don't belittle the difficulty of Hebrew, even if your children were here for some time before starting university. Instead of demeaning English programs or characterizing them as failures for your children, open up discussions about these programs and accept them as legitimate alternatives. If your children choose a course of study that surprises you but they are able to justify that choice based on post-college employment potential, it might be wise to accept their viewpoint as valid. Finally, nearly every Israeli student must have some part-time job to cover rent, food, and other costs. Although there are scholarships to cover nontuition expenses, they often don't cover enough.

9

Building a Life

"What were we thinking? Oh right, we weren't."

—Comedian Extraordinaire Benji Lovitt, from "Becoming Israeli"[1]

If you are dealing with the issues in this chapter, it means you have been in Israel for a while. Congratulations on making it this far, and kudos to the parents and family members who were miles away as their olim relatives muddled through a fairly significant life change. Either way, both parents and olim deserve a round of applause for having made it through the difficult first years.

Whether you completed the IDF or National Service, immigrated with a bachelor's degree after the age of 22, completed your Israeli bachelor's degree a little later, or arrived in Israel with some work experience and a young family in tow, you will soon start to lay the foundation for what will become the rest of your Israeli life. Olim older than age 22 are now young adults, perhaps not all that different from others all over the world looking to find their way.

The same can be said for olim who immigrated in their early 30s looking to settle down with a young family in Israel. All olim must start their career journey; select a community that makes them feel comfortable; develop long-term relationships; establish a family of their own; decide how to afford a home; and, most importantly, continue to foster values that will be a beacon for their lives. These lifecycle events are significant and have as much of a learning curve as other stages previously discussed, with parents continuing to be perplexed by the cultural differences.

Right about now, your aliya journey includes coming in contact with Israelis who feel it is their civic duty to give you advice. They will tell you that you should wear a sweater because it's cold. They will elbow their way past you on a bus or, worse yet, cut you off in traffic and honk incessantly when the light hasn't turned green. They will call you a *frier*, a fool. When you try to offer some sort of rationale or reasoning, regardless of the issue, they won't completely listen and will say *ma ha'kesher,*

Frier
A fool

Ma ha'kesher
Figuratively, "What's your point?" Literally, "How is that connected?"

figuratively meaning "what's your point?" but literally meaning "how is that connected to anything?" Native Israelis might seem peeved that you have benefits that they don't have. When you try to solve a problem or handle a bureaucratic matter, you will find that the phrase *acharei ha'chagim* is a time period—after Sukkot, after Passover, after Independence Day, after Shavot, take your pick. *Acharei ha'chagim* is the reason given, and an accepted one, to push something off. And then there is the time immemorial phrase, "why did you even come here?" as you work your way toward trying to explain that your Zionism got the best of you and you are not a *frier*.

> **Acharei ha'chagim**
> *After the holidays—any holiday really, doesn't matter which one, an acceptable reason to push something off*

Even the most supportive Israelis can't make up for the difficulty of building a life. On your best day, you might get one thing on your "to-do" list done. You might become a slave to the concept of "rinse and repeat," doing the same thing over and over again until you get what you need or solve a particular problem. Supportive friends are helpful, but not much helps when you are frustrated and without family nearby.

As olim begin to fend for themselves in their day-to-day Israeli existence, their level of independence undoubtedly grows, and their parents seem to accept it. Overwhelmingly, both the olim (86%) and the parents (97%) we surveyed agree that after aliya, parents acknowledge that their "new Israeli children" are independent (Figure 1).

Figure 1: After aliya, parents ultimately accept their children's independence

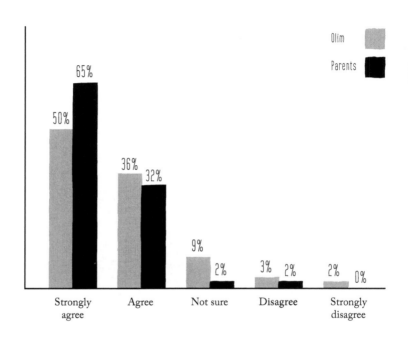

⌀ Reality Check

The reality is that in almost any circumstance, regardless of geographic location, parents of olim have long since lost their ability to influence their children at this age, let alone control them. At best, parents can appeal to their children's sensibilities to take parental advice under consideration. There are some milestone moments for all olim—from employment to home ownership—that we delve into below, and there will be cultural differences between olim and their families, differences that cannot be bridged. The best we can do is highlight some significant milestones for olim; offer some tips; and demystify these concepts for their parents, who find themselves comparing and contrasting "apples and oranges."

Employment

Although some olim come with great skills and well-thought-out plans, many olim know that to succeed in Israel's workplace, they might have to reinvent themselves. It might be as significant as retraining, or it can be marketing themselves to employers in a way Israelis understand. It can mean developing three or four different versions of a resume tailored very specifically to certain postings in a way that will pop out to a human resource manager. As with most things in Israel, finding a job is often about who you know and how your network can help you secure an interview.

Reinventing yourself or hard-core marketing of your skills is a hard thing to do, and not everyone is successful at it. One of us reinvented ourselves at least four times in the past decade since we arrived in Israel, taking on new jobs, learning new skills in Hebrew, and widening and leveraging the knowledge base. But the other one of us never really managed to integrate from a salaried employment perspective. Perhaps it was the age at which we came to Israel; perhaps it's the language skills that make it so tough on older olim.

We would be remiss if we failed to address the elephant in the room when it comes to employment, and that is the commuter parent, the one who gets on a plane and works elsewhere. This is not likely relevant for younger olim, but it might be a consideration for those in their late 20s or 30s with secure jobs outside of Israel. From a tax perspective, olim who work outside of Israel enjoy a 10-year tax reprieve from the Israeli authorities, an exemption from tax and reporting assets and income generated outside of Israel for a decade.[2] It is nevertheless important to get a good handle on tax implications before you travel down the "commuter" road.

Some commuters return home to Israel for weekends, which is more possible if you work in Europe. Others return once a month. And yet, there are others who return once every six weeks, mostly for *chagim* and holiday weekends, as was the case in our home.

Most olim are ready to hustle and climb the Israeli employment ladder no matter how difficult. But we recognize that working outside of Israel has its advantages, and one of them is a steady, reliable, and better income compared with Israeli salaries. It may also be the basis for more family trips "back home." On a lighter note, families don't need to fully convert to Israeli products when one parent can constantly bring things home from outside of Israel.

We are unaware of the statistics regarding olim who work outside of Israel while their families reside in Israel, but we know it is not an uncommon occurrence among American and European olim. In our case, we operated this way for a little more than five and a half years, and it took a significant toll on our family. There is a price to be paid for one parent who is never around. All the parenting and all the responsibilities fall to one person. We had a long-standing tradition of speaking on the telephone every day at 6:00 a.m. Israeli time and 11:00 p.m. Eastern Standard Time. Only one parent knew the ins and outs of daily life in Israel, no matter how often we spoke on the phone. Parents who fly in and out of a child's life can make the family dynamic disorienting. There is a price to be paid for commuting, an unknown one, and it will be a different price for every family. At least be aware of it before you commit to this arrangement.

Chagim
Jewish holidays of all kinds

Here are some tips for olim and parents when it comes to employment. You can cross-reference some of the issues here with those discussed in Chapter 12, "The Path to Financial Literacy":

Tips for Olim	Tips for Parents
It is exceedingly rare to be offered a job before you become a citizen, so don't bank on it.	If your child has not found work before aliya, it is not for want of ambition.
Hebrew is essential to integrate into work life, even in high-tech fields. Go to *ulpan*, don't expect a warm and fuzzy *ulpan* teacher, and be prepared for homework.	Israelis *understand* English, but on the whole, they don't want to converse in it. No sense in trying to convince them otherwise.
Use every connection you know of (*protekzia*) to secure an interview. "Make it on your own" means finding someone you know to help you gain access.	Connections are not frowned on in Israel. If you have friends in Israel, reach out to them. Everyone in Israel knows someone, and it can help.
Social welfare benefits are "richer" than elsewhere in the world, but they come with higher tax rates.	We only refer to our monthly gross pay, and taxes depend on point deductions and pay band.
You get paid in NIS. Try to get used to understanding how far (or not far) that shekel can be stretched.	Avoid the NIS-to-foreign currency conversion because it is not useful to compare. We get paid in NIS and our costs are in NIS.

Tips for Olim

Working part time in one place and part time in another (i.e., 80/20 or 60/40) is common. Make sure to do a *te'um mas* (coordination of income tax) in these cases. It is an authorization by *Mas Hachnasa* to one or more employers as to how much income tax is to be withheld by each from your salary if you work in two places.

If you choose to be a freelancer or are self-employed, you receive zero social benefits—no paid sick leave, vacation, or holidays or payment to a pension or *Bituach Leumi*. Opening up a business has tax implications, and there are online resources to understand them.

"Minus balance" is common. It is pretty simple: you have costs that accrue over the month, but you don't get paid until the 9th of the month, and your costs can be more than your salary. Try to avoid too many *tashlumim*, payments spread out over time without interest, because you will never get a handle on what you owe if everything is on a payment plan.

Tips for Parents

It might seem that your children are piecing together a living. They are. But we have fairly good work environments, like *yemei keif*. Workplaces are family friendly and allow frequent comings and goings because simple milestones, like children entering first grade, are more significant than getting your Ph.D.

Before Rosh Hashana and Passover, there is a *haramat kosit*, a toast for the season, kind of like holiday parties for Christmas and New Year's but for Jewish calendar events. We work to live and do not live to work; maybe that is why we are always ranked as one of the happiest countries in the world.

A negative balance much of the time is an anathema to most people. In Israel, it is common. Food alone is about 20% more in OECD countries.[3] Big box stores don't exist. Don't be surprised if your children only buy fruits or vegetables that are in season. Out of season=insanely expensive. Many Israelis spread out their everyday costs on their credit card *(tashlumim)*, interest free.

Mas Hachnasa
Income Tax Authority

Yemei keif
Fun days

Haramat kosit
Toast

Tashlumim
Payment plan to spread out payments for a given purchase, normally without "rib-it," interest

Tips for Olim

The Israeli workplace is family friendly, and you will find your employer quite accommodating. However, children have more vacation days than you do, and finding childcare is a major challenge for working households. It is common for daycare centers to close for several weeks in August, causing parents angst and the need to arrange alternative care by family members, friends, or babysitters or use vacation days.[4]

Know your rights; learn them from friends, co-workers, websites (Kol Zchut is an excellent one), and Facebook groups. You might get burned once or twice.

Tips for Parents

It is far easier for Israelis to take vacation during Jewish holidays.[5] It is also widely accepted to take family vacations in the summer. But it is far more difficult to take off from work during what is perceived as the largest productive stretch of the year, October to April (after Sukkot and until Pesach). If you come to visit during this period, your grandchildren will be in school and your children will be working.[6]

If something seems off to you, see if you can find someone you know in Israel to help. Adopted families are generally a good resource if you have access to them.

Community and Relationships

When we arrived in Israel, we had just celebrated our 20th wedding anniversary. We didn't have a large group of friends in the United States, but we knew we would miss the ones we had. Because we came for a pilot year, we knew we wanted to live in Jerusalem. We liked urban life, and our community in south Jerusalem was—and still is—known to be one of the more open, tolerant, and pluralistic ones left in the city. The neighborhood is close to bus lines, so we didn't have a car for a few years. Our neighborhood is known to have quite a high percentage of English speakers, but that was not the reason we "landed" here. We simply liked the area. It is conveniently located near schools and public transportation, we began making friends here in our pilot year, and it combined a certain degree of quaintness with urban living.

We learned quite early that many Israelis are separated by one degree of separation. Even for those who were born to olim parents and spoke English at home, the smallness of the country guaranteed some connectedness. They served in the army together, they were in kindergarten together, their brothers and sisters were in youth movement together, their cousins dated in university, and so on. It is hard to compete with that level of intimacy, and if you also lack cultural references (which many olim do), you find it hard to find commonality with people in your community. Ultimately, we created our own community, inviting tourists, students, lone soldiers, and many more to our home for Shabbat. In essence, our home *became* our community, and it has remained that way ever since.

Some olim look to their local synagogues as their "community" and are disappointed. There is a good reason for this. Synagogues, Jewish Federations, and Jewish community centers take on a central and identity-level role in the Diaspora. They become the place where you connect with others as Jews, or connect for Jewish causes, or for pro-Israel causes. In Israel, we are all Jews. Synagogues in Israel are not the center of action; they often lack official rabbis, and there is one for *every* kind of Jew in any neighborhood. Our community centers *(matnasim)* are quasi-political institutions with events that range from after-school activities to social welfare causes.

To put a more positive spin on it, we aren't part of *any* group because we belong to *every* group. We are part of a larger whole, a messy Jewish community that takes up an entire nation.[7]

As discussed more fully in the final chapter of this book,

do not to underestimate the importance of community and the sense of loneliness without friends. Olim lack extended family and rely on a community to make up for that solitude. If you can't find your bearings within a community, it might be very hard to culturally adjust. Here are some tips we found helpful after more than 10 years in Israel:

Tips for Olim

Single olim tend to band together and reside in communities that suit them and offer a support network.

Common language and cultural experiences make it easier for immigrants to be in relationships with one another.

Israeli weddings, bar mitzvahs, and other occasions are quite informal events, often without ties or jackets or long gowns. And they are nearly always planned at the last minute.

If you came to Israel as a young married couple, you might find your new living arrangements to be somewhat of a downgrade.

Tips for Parents

Communities are different than what you are used to. When you see your children's living arrangement for the first time, remember the phrase, "If you're happy, I'm happy."

Get to know whom your child is dating. It might be a pure-bred Israeli, which means a cultural adjustment for you.

You will not likely succeed in convincing your children to buck this informal trend. Attire for these events might even be shorts and sandals. Best get used to it.

Remember the phrase, "If you're happy, I'm happy," and don't be surprised by the lack of appropriate infrastructure.

Tips for Olim

If you have children, research residential areas that suit educational or child care needs while also considering commuting distances to work.

Most couples cannot afford more than one car, hence the need to be in close proximity to efficient public transportation.

Tips for Parents

Latchkey children are common. Elementary school ends early, and your children will always be scrambling to find after-school arrangements.

If you live in a suburb with a two-car garage, it will be hard to understand the importance of public transportation.

Homeownership

We rented an apartment for our first year, an arrangement we made on a quick one-week trip a few months before aliya. Once we settled in, we started looking for apartments in certain areas of our neighborhood. We were incredibly lucky to have sold our home in the United States six months after our aliya and to have found a home in Jerusalem that same month. We flipped a large home in the United States for our beautiful albeit smaller Jerusalem home, and we would not have it any other way.

Homeownership is one of the toughest milestones for both native-born Israelis and olim alike, although native Israelis seem to know how difficult it is to purchase a home, and an entire subculture has developed around Israeli parents helping their children purchase their first apartment.

Thoroughly research mortgages and rights related to them. Laws change frequently; we advise delving deep into what kind of discounts you are truly entitled to and whether it is even worth the hassle applying for them.

Here are some suggestions to guide you through some of the homeownership landscape:

Tips for Olim	Tips for Parents
All Israelis find the purchase of a home or an apartment onerous.[8] Olim are eligible for certain loan benefits when seeking a mortgage, but most are still required to come up with a 30% or 40% down payment.	This is an unfortunate reality for *all* Israelis. If you can help your children toward the purchase of their first apartment, it will be of significant help to them.
You might be renting for a long period of time. It might not be a bad thing, since you can try out new communities and not be tied down to one place. Most rentals come quite bare, and you might find yourself moving your oven or air-conditioner from place to place. The only downside is moving costs.	Rental costs are relatively low compared to the U.S. or other countries, thus it's reasonable to rent for an extended period. Make sure your children have their rental contract reviewed by someone who understands it. You might need to find someone to be a guarantor on the contract, just in case there is default on the rent.
Buying on paper can appear to be less costly but is incredibly time consuming, you might not get what you expected, and it still might cost more.	Buying on paper might seem to be a more financially sound idea, but it isn't always. You must pay for a good portion of the home long before you get a set of keys, locking up your money for some time.

10

Coming With Kids

"And will you succeed?
Yes! You will, indeed!
98 and ¾ percent guaranteed.
Kid, You'll Move Mountains."

—Dr. Seuss, *Oh the Places You'll Go*[1]

It is often said, and we agree, that the younger you are when you arrive in Israel, the greater chance you have at success. While there is no hard and fast rule or cutoff date, if you have young children and are considering aliya, suffice it to say that it is best to make the move by, the latest, the end of their primary school years. The closer they get to middle school (7th grade), the harder it is to acclimate linguistically and socially.

Let's start by focusing on olim with young children, from infancy through 6th grade. From 7th grade onward, educational frameworks are somewhat more complicated in terms of nonlocal choices and preparation for the *bagrut* matriculation exams later in high school, which we discuss later in this chapter.

Primary school starts on September 1 and finishes on June 30. The calendar cutoff for first-graders might be different than in your home country, so please check to make sure that your child meets that cutoff. Children go to school six days a week, Sundays through Fridays, until middle or high school, when many have Fridays off. Jewish holidays are official vacation days, as are the days before the holiday, *erev chag.* The most intensive learning happens in the six-month period after Sukkot in the fall until Passover in the spring. Anything that falls before or after that time period is light on academics and heavy on ceremonies and parties. Purim, for example, which usually falls in March, is officially a one-day holiday on the Jewish calendar. In Israel, it appears to have been extended to two weeks, with fairs, dress-up days, and more—a two-week ramp-up to Purim itself. After Passover, there are the *chagim leumi'im,* national holidays like Holocaust Remembrance Day, Memorial Day, and Independence Day, followed by Shavuot—all within the span of a few weeks.

Going into first grade is more celebrated than becoming

Bagrut
High school exams, in 11th and 12th grades, that are required to receive a high school matriculation degree

Erev chag
Day before any holiday, when there is normally no school

Chagim leumi'im
National holidays within one week that fall right after Passover: Holocaust Remembrance Day, Memorial Day, and Independence Day

Shalom kita aleph
Ceremonies held around the country on the Shabbat before children start first grade, which is more important than their college graduation

a doctor or getting a Ph.D. *Shalom kita aleph,* or "Welcome to first grade" events, are held in every community on the Shabbat before first grade begins. Every child starting first grade is singled out, goodie bags are distributed to them, and special speeches are given in their honor—like a commencement speech but for six-year-olds. All 120 members of Knesset, the President of the State of Israel, ministers, and mayors fan out all over the country to greet first graders on their first day of school—which, by the way, is over by about 11:00 a.m. to give the children a chance to adjust, as if eight weeks of summer vacation weren't enough.

If you are a family that managed with one working parent before aliya, financially that is much more difficult in Israel. Israeli families generally include two working parents, which strains every single young family in Israel. Although there are very "rich" and family friendly maternity and paternity leave policies, after four months, parents put their babies into day care centers, and by age two, nearly every child is in some form of preschool. If you send your child to a private kindergarten, it will no doubt be more expensive than the public school system.

The public school system is arranged, more or less, by district. If you live within certain boundaries, schools in that area are automatically available to you, which means that schools must make room for your child if you live in that area. Should you choose a school that is outside of your school district, you will likely have to appeal to local education officials within the municipality, and there is no guarantee that you will succeed inasmuch as schools first serve those within their district. Please know that you might not get your first choice of schools in the year after you make aliya, particularly if you were not in Israel to weave through and fight the system to get what you want.

Those who send their children to private schools where tuition costs are high will find the Israeli school system significantly cheaper. News flash; it isn't free. Elementary school is about NIS 3,400 per year and high school can go as high as NIS 15,000 per year. The basic school system has some costs, and parents might have to pay for schoolbooks. Every year, the Ministry of Education requires that elementary and high schools publish a list of expenses parents will incur. These expenses are approved by the Ministry and some, similar to bank charges, might not make sense to you. Worse yet is that these costs fail to include a whole host of other random expenses, like gifts for teachers, gifts for students, trips, celebratory lunches, and year-end parties. These are in addition to the after-school costs for *chugim* and *tzaharon*, after-school activities that every parent will need if they want to work a full day.

All children must be registered with the local municipality and, as with all Israeli bureaucracy, you will be hard-pressed to find them speaking English. There will be forms in Hebrew, questions in Hebrew, clerks who speak way too fast in Hebrew, and principals who might want to interview your young children in Hebrew when they don't speak a word of it. If you feel you are in over your head, see if you can get assistance from someone in your local area.

And speaking of Hebrew, when we made aliya, school administrators encouraged you to send your children to *ulpan* outside of school hours and outside of the school building. Today, this is less common and every school ought to have a *morah or rakaz l'olim*, a coordinator/teacher for new immigrants who is required to evaluate your children and take them out of class to help them with Hebrew. Show up in school on the very first day (September 1) and make sure that the coordinator, teachers, and principals know you will be hounding them for a tutoring schedule. Don't fall for the *acharei hachagim* line because it will be Hanukah before it is taken care of.

Chugim
In this context, after-school activities

Tzaharon
After-school activities for younger children, sometimes within the school building itself

---

Morah or rakaz l'olim
Teacher/ coordinator in school who is required to assist new immigrants

---

Acharei hachagim
"After the holidays," which more or less means anytime after Sukkot but before Passover, or any time immediately following any holiday, large or small

Tilboshet achida
School uniform

M'gamot
Electives that you take starting in 10th grade

Y'chidot
Number of points for each high school course, ranging from three to five points

Bagruyot
Matriculation exams that start in 11th grade and go through the end of 12th

Mo'ed bet
"Do-over" test in case you don't do well enough on the first exam

Tz'yun magen
Overall score for the year before the bagrut exam

Uniforms *(tilboshet achida)* might not be what you are used to. They are T-shirts with an ironed-on symbol for the school. You are instructed to buy them in a specific store, and all those stores will have your school logo to iron on. In most schools, shorts, jeans, and cargo pants are allowed, even as part of the uniform. A word to the wise: get a bunch of white shirts and blue pants or skirts. White shirts and blue pants are the uniform of choice for school ceremonies, and you will need many of them. You can't go wrong with having enough white shirts. We didn't know how important this was until our son was nearly sent home from school for not wearing one for Memorial Day ceremonies.

As for high school, depending on where you live, high school starts either in 7th or 9th grade. In Jerusalem, elementary school is 1st through 6th. There used to be a time when invasive testing for high school was allowed. It isn't any longer, although there are still interviews conducted by principals and teachers. In most cities, you register online for high school and prioritize selection of the top three to four schools. In general, the high schools you choose are not likely to be near your home, which means your children will be taking public buses, scooters, or bicycles to get to and from school. The Moovit app was never more important if you want to ensure that your high schooler makes it to class on time.

The most important terms to know for parents of high school children are *m'gamot*, electives that you take starting in 10th grade; *y'chidot*, the number of points for each high school course ranging from three to five points; *bagruyot*, matriculation exams that start in 11th grade and go through the end of 12th; *mo'ed bet*, the "do-over" test in case you don't do well enough on the first exam; and *tz'yun magen*, the overall score for the year *before* the *bagrut* exam.

Don't forget that olim have rights when it comes to high

school exams and *bagruyot*. They range from extra points on the final grade to having the test read to them to receiving a special test only for olim in that subject. Those rights are available for 10 years. Make sure you are aware of your children's rights, know the pros and cons of each option, and receive information in writing. If your children do not receive their rights and you become aware of them after high school, it becomes nearly impossible to retroactively exercise those rights.

Families who opted for soft landings in English-speaking communities might find that their children struggle when they get to high school. "Street Hebrew," or "youth movement Hebrew," is not sufficient for the *bagrut* system and, to do well, they will need very high-level language skills. Children who muddled through or performed academically and linguistically well in 5th-9th grades might find it quite difficult when they get to 10th grade and find that their Hebrew is insufficient. Some children seek an English-only high school, and there are some available in Israel, or they might want to return to schools they did well in "back at home." Be prepared for the difficulties high school can bring, and consider private tutors, yet another added expense borne even by native Israelis.

Some ever-resourceful olim who struggled with trying to understand the education system established educational consultancy businesses. If you are having a hard time finding the right choices for your family, paying a consultant to help you, particularly one that speaks your actual and cultural language, can go a long way. Consultants can be particularly helpful for special education needs, but please secure recommendations before you sign up with any consultant.

⮂ The Dialogue

Olim with young families can hear a range of concerns from parents about the future of their grandchildren who are being uprooted to a new school system:

Oleh
Parent

"Turns out we will need to supplement their learning with outside tutors. It is quite common."

"Why? Doesn't the school cover the basic information needed?"

"The kids are taking *mo'ed bet*, so we won't be able to visit until late July."

"*Mo'ed bet?* They didn't do well enough the first time around? Did they fail?"

"We decided the experimental school is best for our kids."

"They aren't going to have a set curriculum or tests or grades? What kind of school is that?"

We were able to spend a pilot year here and enrolled our children in local schools, and it gave us the ability to make a more informed choice once we made aliya. Yet, we had to fight hard to get our children into local schools. Most principals do not see an advantage to investing in a child whose family is here for a pilot year, and they would rather make the seat "available" for a child who will remain a student in the school for the long haul. Don't expect teachers or school administrators to be very helpful during a pilot year, but as a parent, it will help if you learn more about your options. A pilot year isn't an option for every family; so, for this reason, we thought it might be helpful to outline some of the educational choices facing olim.

The educational sector in Israel is divided into four groups: the *Mamlachti* system for secular families, the *Mamlachti Dati* system for the Orthodox, the *Haredi* system for the ultra-Orthodox, and the Arab system for Arab citizens of Israel and east Jerusalem residents. The east Jerusalem education system is divided into four separate elements, and for many reasons not discussed here, it is far more complicated than the *Haredi* education system, which is a frequently raised issue on Israel's public agenda.

Much is written about the school system in Israel—how segmented it is and how limited the choices can be. For example, those who self-identify as ultra-Orthodox might find the *Haredi* school system in Israel far too restrictive for them. The *Haredi* school system overall is not at all similar to Jewish day schools outside of Israel, so be prepared for the stark differences.

The *Haredi* school system for boys, for example, does not teach any secular subjects after 3rd grade—no math, English, or Hebrew language, only religious subjects. Virtually no graduate from the ultra-Orthodox system has a matriculation degree at the end of high school, which is sorely needed for

Mamlachti
State secular school

Mamlachti Dati
State religious school

Haredi
"Trembling" before God, referring to the ultra-Orthodox, some of whom do not consider themselves Zionist

Hardal
Haredi
Leumi,
those who
are more
aligned with
ultra-Ortho-
dox lifestyles
but who
are more
Zionistic and
nationalistic

higher education. Very few *Haredim* serve in the Israeli army, despite many efforts to draft them. And finally, those who identify with the ultra-Orthodox lifestyle can choose to send their children to a *Hardal* school, *Haredi-Leumi* schools that separate boys and girls; have more frontal teaching hours for religious subjects; have a full secular education curriculum; and consider themselves Zionists and dedicated to the country's security, thus drafting into IDF units.

Regarding *Haredi* schools for girls, while some do have matriculation degrees, they are very limited in their scope. Few complete high-level math that is now expected in Israel. Very few have access to high school electives in computers, cyber, or any STEM subject—again, something that has grown in popularity.

The *Mamlachti Dati* schools come in all shapes and sizes. Some maintain separation between boys and girls; others don't. Israeli families who might not adhere strictly to religious law— for example, traveling on Shabbat—might send their children to these schools so that they are at least exposed to these issues. The curriculum is largely set by the Ministry of Education, and schools are highly supervised by the Ministry, something that is not done at all in the *Haredi* system. Nearly all graduates of these schools end up with matriculation high school degrees, and most either serve in the IDF or do National Service. This is the system that is most similar to Jewish day schools in North America, with two major differences: it is cheaper in Israel, and the school days are a lot shorter, which makes it very difficult on working families.

Kfiya datit
Religious
coercion in
the school
system

There is a significant public debate particularly over the *Mamlachti* secular school system. Many in Israel assert that too many religious issues and religious texts have creeped their way into the secular school curriculum, against parental wishes. It is a concept known colloquially as *kfiya datit,* forcing religiosity on those who don't want it. Without delving into the complicated debate surrounding this issue, it is important to know that students attending these schools continue to have vacations on Jewish holidays; they continue to learn the historical and biblical connection to the State of Israel; and, even in high school, there is a minimal requirement to take Bible-related matriculation exams.

There are some "specialty" schools in Israel, and all of them are under the Ministry of Education supervision. They include, for example, the network of TALI schools, which focuses on an egalitarian Jewish curriculum; the Max Rayne School, Hand in Hand for Bilingual Education (Yad b'Yad), where Jews and Arabs learn in joint classrooms and in two languages simultaneously; the Democratic or Experimental Schools, where there are no grades or formal class environments; the Na'ale School, for olim in high school who came to Israel without parents; the Steiner/Waldorf schools, which focus on interdisciplinary learning; and the Jerusalem Academy for Music and Dance, for gifted students in high school. There are many other network-type specialty schools, some for elementary and some only for high school, and Nefesh B'Nefesh will either have or can direct you to information that can be of assistance to you.

From day care through elementary school, the school day is short, with most schools finishing by 2:00 p.m. or sometimes earlier. It is for this reason that many parents select fairly expensive after-school activities to keep their children busy until they come home from work. Grandparents are significant parts of a nuclear family, and they often pick children up from kindergarten or elementary school and ferry them to other activities. To put it simply, the educational system depends on grandparents, yet olim come to Israel without that net. Mainly for this reason, one of us took a job that was two blocks from our son's school, and we largely stayed in Jerusalem for employment to manage child care. Under Israeli law, after age 9, children can walk to school without a parent, and once they get to that age, they shuttle themselves around, they become latchkey children, and they buy their own snacks from the local *makolet*.

One might wonder, for instance, why Tuesdays are always shorter school days. No matter where you are in the country, school ends early on Tuesday because it is *tnuat no'ar* youth movement day, the official day of the week when kids get out early from school (as early as 1:00 p.m.) and walk themselves to some decrepit building, where activities are "organized" by kids who are around age 15. Soon after the Sukkot holiday, youth groups have a whole month dedicated to bringing in "new recruits" (i.e., the younger children in 3rd grade) and giving new *shevet* (tribe) names for the ones who "graduate out" in 10th or 11th grade. There are bonfires; long nights; and even a *laila lavan*, a white night where the kids are up all night. The holiday of Lag Ba'Omer is a scary combination of all-night bonfires "supervised" by teenagers. Then there is the *bayit rek* concept, where parents leave an empty house and a bunch of kids hang out doing what we are told are all very safe and responsible activities. This is just the way it is, and all you can do as a parent is make sure that they are safe as can be.

Although all youth groups (Tzofim, Bnei Akiva, Hashomer Ha'Tzair, and Ezra) are conducted in Hebrew and led by other very young children, some are more experiential (less language-based) like Sayarot, which focuses on hiking, and the Zoo Patrol, affiliated with Jerusalem's Tisch Family Zoological Gardens Noah program, which includes work with animals at the zoo. No matter what program your child participates in, youth movements are of significant social value and are strong influencing factors for kids through their teenage years. Children end up spending many after-school hours with their youth groups.

Makolet
Small neighborhood hole-in-the-wall supermarket

Tnuat no'ar
Youth groups

Laila lavan
White nights, pretty much staying up all night

Bayit rek
Empty house without parents, which immediately triggers a request for friends to hang out at the empty house

Because of the short school day and the need for grandparent assistance, educational choices will often be an anchor issue for where a family decides to put down roots. Ideally, a family with children would like to live within walking distance of an appropriate school and of the *matnas*, the local community hub where after-school activities take place and where kids can "hang out" under watchful eyes.

⊘ Reality Check

The reality is that there is far less parental helicoptering than there is outside of Israel, and most Israeli parents look forward to the day when their children achieve latchkey status so they themselves can work a full day. It is a good reason for young families to test out communities simply for their educational value before permanently putting down roots. If you are fairly happy with your educational options in your home country, the Israeli system might not meet your expectations, but no school is perfect. One of our pet peeves is the history curriculum in primary school years, where the only history taught is Jewish history. At first, that might sound appealing, until you realize it excludes *all other* history. As for Hebrew language skills, we strongly suggest that you throw children into the deep end when it comes to immersion, particularly if they are age 12 or younger. They will learn faster from their friends than they ever will from a teacher.

Rabbi Dr. Michael Reichel, the principal of Chorev Middle School in Jerusalem and an educational professional, has seen many children struggle through their first few years in Israel. According to Reichel, if one lands in an English-speaking community, within one year, children understand 80% of Hebrew conversation (receptive language skills) and are

Matnas
Mercaz l'tarbut, nofesh v'sport, a local community center (every community has one) for culture, leisure, and sports

able to communicate 40% of the time in Hebrew. By Passover of year 2, children have 100% receptive language and 80% speaking skills, yet language acquisition continues through university. These statistics improve if there is full immersion in a Hebrew-speaking community. Don't underestimate how hard high school can be from a linguistic standpoint, even if you have been in Israel for a few years. Tutors are an option worth considering, and always remember that the education system offers olim certain rights—know them well, and secure confirmation in writing.

☐ Reframing Educational Options

🕊 **Olim with Children:** If at all possible, consider a pilot year or even a six-month period. During your pilot period, enroll your children in a school that would be under your consideration, and live near the school so you can see how your children navigate it. It can help you make a more informed decision. If you can't spend that amount of time in Israel, at least make a trip with your kids so that you have the time to scout schools within communities under your consideration. Ask questions, and post in Facebook groups. Be prepared to deal with municipal representatives who have control over where you send your children to school. You will experience teachers who are dealing with large classes and don't necessarily slow down for your children, but believe in many WhatsApp groups and you might lose control of them. In general, the educational atmosphere in primary school appears to be a little more lax than it is in other countries, on the theory that high school is that much more pressured. Finally, appreciate that within a few short months, your children will probably have vastly improved Hebrew, it will be better than yours, they will blend their English and Hebrew all the time, they will pick up unwanted Israeli mannerisms that you might have to discourage, but otherwise they will advance faster than you can imagine.

Grandparents of Olim: You will be astounded by the amount of Jewish history and texts your grandchildren know, regardless of the type of school they attend. Their school year will run on a Jewish calendar, they will be trained on the importance of community service, they will be exposed to Jews with origins from all over the globe, and they will have cultural days that honor the multiethnicity in Israel. They will be dedicated to the country, and you will see it in how your grandchildren bow their heads with utmost seriousness on Memorial Day and, 24 hours later, dance in the streets with Israeli flags on Independence Day. They will be fiercely independent, they will demonstrate little fear, they will have chutzpah, and they will likely be political even at a young age. They will use phrases like *m'shoah l'tekuma*, "from the Holocaust to rebirth," and their patriotism will be infectious.

Constructive Dialogue

Olim
"Schools are very different. I will try and explain it all."

Parents
"Whatever you decide is best. We trust you."

11

Circle of Life: Grandparents on Down Through Grandchildren

"Absence Makes the Heart Grow Fonder" or
"Out of Sight, Out of Mind?"

If you are a young family who lives within minimal driving distance from your parents/grandparents, or if you have the opportunity to create holiday and weekend get-togethers with relatively limited travel, moving to Israel will dent family cohesiveness. You also are not likely to see each other for every birth, bar mitzvah, bat mitzvah, wedding, or birthday milestone. Choices will have to be made because you simply cannot "jump the pond" to visit family as often as you'd like.

There is no question that air travel was easier prior to COVID-19. Yet, even before the global pandemic disrupted our ability to hop on planes, grandchildren who live far away from grandparents begin a long-distance relationship when families make aliya. No matter how often you think you will travel, it will likely be too infrequent to bridge gaps that may develop between grandchildren and grandparents or among other family members who can vie for your time when your visit is only a few weeks.

Once parents settle down to an Israeli routine, jobs get in the way. Once children settle down in the educational system, school schedules get in the way. Before you know it, Israeli grandchildren have schedules of their own. They might even be unwilling to travel during certain times of the year. Ours, for instance, don't like to be anywhere else other than Israel for the holidays. It is easier to take children out of their educational frameworks before high school, but once they reach 11th and 12th grades, *bagrut* season in the spring takes hold. When grandchildren are in the army, they need permission from the IDF to leave the country, and many don't go.

School vacations are tied to the Jewish calendar. Rosh Hashana, Yom Kippur, and Sukkot are often referred to as *chagei Tishrei,* inasmuch as they fall within the Jewish month of Tishrei. It isn't a good time to be traveling outside of Israel because children will have just started school, but it is a good

Bagrut
Matric-ulation exam time period that often starts right after Passover and can continue through mid-July in 11th and 12th grades

Chagei Tishrei
All of the holidays that fall during the Jewish month of Tishrei —Rosh Hashana, Yom Kippur, and Sukkot

time for grandparents to visit for an extended period.

The next big block of quality time available for grandparents and grandchildren is Hanukah. It might fall over the Christmas holidays but it might not. Israeli children have off from school on Hanukah, but their parents do not have off from work. Again, it is another great opportunity for grandparents to visit and spend time with their grandchildren.

Passover, which falls either in March or April, is closer to a two-week school vacation. It is an opportunity to travel to family outside of Israel but, as we indicated, beware of Israeli grandchildren who will not want to leave during this period. This is the third block of quality time for grandparents and their Israeli grandchildren.

The summer months (July and August) are the most appropriate time for travel overseas, at least in relation to the children's school schedules. Prior to high school, most children finish school by July 1 and start again on September 1, leaving them with plenty of time off. Although there are Israeli summer camps in July, August is a time when most Israeli parents struggle to find frameworks that are available all month long. It is a good time to visit family outside of Israel, but parents would be thrilled if grandparents would come to Israel for grandparent-led summer camp, particularly when parents don't have enough vacation time for a whole month off.

We recognize that these blocks of time don't necessarily work for every set of grandparents, particularly those who are still employed, have other grandchildren to visit, or are otherwise committed such that they must juggle their schedule to fit with their Israeli family's time off. All we can say is that the grandparent-grandchild relationship is a precious one and requires effort to nurture it across the geographical divide.

ᯓ The Dialogue

We often forget that the decision to make aliya affects the grandparent-grandchild relationship as much as the parent-child relationship. We are blessed to live in an era where communication is far easier and cheaper than it once was. FaceTime, WhatsApp video, Facebook video, Viber, Skype, Zoom, and more technologies are being developed every day. But no matter what video or communication advancement comes next, they hardly replace real face time when grandchildren are still infants or toddlers.

Breaking the news that a young family is making aliya with children in tow raises all sorts of emotions, including fear of abandonment and loss of meaningful contact. The conversation can go something like this:

Oleh	Parents

"I promise I will be here when you need me."

"That's what you say now."

"We will video chat all the time."

"We are not that good with technology."

"Come to us for the holidays and summers."

"We have other children and grandchildren, and it's too hot there."

If you accept the notion that encouraging grandchildren to call their grandparents doesn't always work and that time zones can adversely impact communication, parents should find ways to keep grandparents relevant. Parents who have moved their children far away from grandparents might benefit from talking about family history, mentioning funny stories, and finding ways to work grandparents into conversations so that they can remain relevant to their Israeli grandchildren. It isn't always easy, but it might keep that quality connection strong enough until families can meet again either in Israel or "back home."

And then there is the sandwich generation, those of us with young children *and* with parents who slowly get to old age without us. Young olim cannot possibly understand the emotional depth of this issue at the time they board a plane to make aliya. And perhaps parents of olim don't realize it either. But the time comes when you must juggle your job and children in Israel while dealing with parents in another time zone that need our attention. In our case, one parent had a stroke, and there was a 16-month absence with our family in Israel to deal with issues in the United States. No one wants to think about any of these matters at the time of aliya, but they are on the horizon, along with the guilt that comes with them.

If you are lucky enough to have family who is prepared to travel to Israel or vice versa for family occasions, circle-of-life events demonstrate the cultural differences that develop between families who live in Israel and those who remain in the Diaspora.

It is fair to say that marriages and bar/bat mitzvahs in Israel are important, but it bears repeating that they are quite informal events. No suits or ties or gowns or high heels. Attendance at these events requires at best a clean white shirt and nice pants or a simple dress. Sometimes it can be jeans and sandals. At weddings, there really isn't anything like "walking down the aisle," because there barely is an aisle at all. People just tend to congregate in a group. Don't be surprised if events are held in a forest or in the desert and food is served informally, buffet style. And don't forget that the *lingu franca* is Hebrew, which means that speeches and videos will not be done in English. As time goes on, olim families traveling to events outside of the country begin to feel the culture shock of the formality they shed when they became Israelis.

Finally, a word about life cycle events in Israel, specifically marriage and divorce. We would be remiss if we failed to note the role of the *Rabbanut,* which comes into play when olim are getting married or divorced.

In case you were not aware, there is no separation of "church and state" in Israel, an issue that garners significant public attention among Israelis. It is a complicated subject, but for the purposes of this chapter, suffice it to say that the *Rabbanut* has a significant hold on major life-cycle events, including marriages and divorces. The *Rabbanut* is Orthodox, and the standard of "Jewishness" for marriage is different than the standard for making aliya.

As most olim recall, part of the aliya paperwork includes a document establishing their Jewish lineage. Any Jew from anywhere in the world has a right to claim Israeli citizenship based on the 1950 Right of Return law called *Chok HaShvut.* It grants every Jew, wherever they may be, the right to come to Israel as an immigrant and become an Israeli citizen. To claim that right, you complete a form, get a letter from your rabbi, and submit the paperwork to the appropriate authorities. Since 1970, the right to immigrate under this law has been extended to include the children and grandchildren of a Jew and their spouses. For practical purposes, this means that you don't need to prove that you are matrilineally Jewish to make aliya and become a citizen. The purpose of the 1970 amendment was

---

Rabbanut
Rabbinate of the State of Israel

Chok HaShvut
1950s law called the Right of Return that grants every Jew, everywhere, the right to become an Israeli citizen

Halacha
Jewish law as interpreted by Orthodox rabbis

essentially to apply the same standard as Germany's Nurenberg Laws, to wit, Nurenberg did not use a religious law definition of who is a Jew, and therefore the Law of Return's definition for citizenship eligibility does not follow *halacha.*

But that is not the case when it comes to marriage, particularly if you want your marriage to be recognized by the state. There is only one kind of state-approved Jewish marriage in Israel and that is under *Rabbanut* auspices, which is Orthodox. The *Rabbanut* follows Jewish law, which only recognizes as Jewish those whose mothers are Jews or who themselves converted to Judaism under approved authorities. Couples can only be married by rabbis approved by the Rabbinate, and women are required to attend family purity classes. Civil marriages performed outside of Israel are recognized for purposes of national statistics but not personal status. Similarly, "common law" marriages afford couples some marriage-related rights and protections but not full recognition. Many religious and nonreligious couples avoid dealing with the *Rabbanut* by getting married outside of Israel or having a friend (or even an Orthodox rabbi who might not be approved by it) officiate, if nothing else to protest what they perceive as the social injustice of the *Rabbanut* system. There is also an organization called Tzohar that accompanies couples through the marriage process to avoid as much of the *Rabbanut* frustration as possible.

Without delving in too deeply to the socio-political-religious issues that are part and parcel of the *Rabbanut* and its position of authority in Israel, the *Rabbanut* has been making it harder and harder for immigrants to prove they are Jews, and there are organizations that can help you navigate the situation when the time comes.[1] You may have to provide documentation showing that your parents' marriage was in accordance with Jewish law or, if you are a convert, further evidence that the conversion was in accordance with *halacha.*

Divorce is no easier. Both rabbinical and family courts are authorized to adjudicate issues involving divorce between Jewish couples. The legal venue that handles the dispute is fixed according to where the issue was first petitioned. It has created venue shopping, a situation where one spouse can preempt the other—for instance, filing in the rabbinical court so that rabbinical judges have the authority to adjudicate all the issues. The controlling legal venue is the one which was first approached. The results affect child custody and support and division of property. Some cases involve the refusal of husbands to give wives a Jewish writ of divorce, leaving them in purgatory, unable to divorce or remarry according to Jewish law.

The societal issues that arise from the *Rabbanut* system are beyond the scope of this book, but olim should understand the system so that they manage within it—that is, should they choose to be recognized as married or divorced by the State of Israel.

☑ Reality Check

The circle of life in Israel can take olim through marriage, sometimes divorce, but definitely through long-distance relationships between grandchildren and grandparents. The State of Israel that considered you Jewish enough to become a citizen and defend the country is the very same one that won't hesitate to question your Jewishness at the time of your marriage or divorce.

Under all circumstances, the grandparents-grandchildren connection is something that is difficult to maintain or develop when faced with time zone and scheduling challenges. Parents should actively try and bridge the gaps between grandparents and grandchildren or else out of sight will definitely mean out of mind. Despite the ease of communication, grandchildren might not communicate as often as we'd like. Some of it is because of the generational digital divide, some of it is because of the time difference. Communications dwindle largely because grandchildren begin to develop their own schedules and don't really manage to make their grandparent conversations part of their weekly or even monthly routine. Despite Wi-Fi, video chat, Facetime, Skype, and text messaging, weeks can slip by with minimal contact if parents don't try to reinforce that this relationship is a cherished one. The grandparent-grandchild relationship needs more active nurturing, and everyone involved will have to work harder to maintain the connection between generations.

☐ Reframing the Absence Gap

🕊 **Olim who are parents:** When you boarded a plane to Israel, you took your born and unborn children away from their grandparents. If you had the privilege of growing up with an extended family nearby, you will miss it more than you even know. You will miss calling on a grandparent to help with a sick child or quick trips to the pizza store. You will miss the "secret sauce" that exists between grandchildren and grandparents. It is not going to be easy to balance your job, your family, and your parents who are far away. There is no sugar coating it. If the relationship between your parents and your children is important to you, you will have to work hard to develop and maintain meaningful relationships between grandparents and grandchildren. Talk about grandparents and your family in your home to "keep the flame alive." Plan to visit when you can, or plan to have parents visit at times when kids are off from school. Finally, prepare for the day when you and your aging parents will be separated by a plane flight. It won't be easy, you might be wracked by guilt, but some of it will be assuaged if you give some thought to how you plan to manage the sandwich generation when the time comes.

Grandparents of olim: When your children boarded a plan to make aliya, they took away your grandchildren, the born and the unborn. It will be impossible to explain how you feel to your children. They won't understand until they are grandparents themselves, and that might be years away. If your relationship with your grandchildren is important to you, do the very best you can to maximize their vacation time with you—either in Israel or in your home. We didn't sugar coat it for the parents, and we won't for you either. If you want to develop and maintain a strong connection with your grandchildren, it will take more work than if they were closer. At the end of the day, it is worth it.

Constructive Dialogue

Olim
"Let's try and plan when we will see each other. What if we schedule a set time to talk?"

Parents
"Maybe we can get someone to help with the digital stuff so we can see our grandchildren. What time works best for them?"

12

The Path to Financial Literacy

"Financial literacy: the ability to understand the basic principles of business and personal finance."

—Cambridge Dictionary[1]

All olim, regardless of age, are faced with a financial system that is truly foreign to them not just because of the language barrier. Israel's financial system, from personal banking to pension funds to opening a small business, is rife with bureaucratic idiosyncrasies that are probably unique to every country. To manage in Israel, immigrants must navigate these systems all while learning new Hebrew terms. For young olim, many of these financial concepts would have been new to them even in their native countries.

This chapter is a reality check of how daily life is managed in Israel. Suffice it to say that learning it all requires experience, living in Israel long enough to get burned, and knowing how to improve the next time. The topics we address here are applicable to olim of all ages.

Some of the material here is repeated from other chapters because we felt it important to centralize financial information in one place. There are plenty of resources on the subjects we cover here, and we encourage olim to post in Facebook groups, in addition to looking up Nefesh B'Nefesh's website,[2] which offers some sample budgets for different age groups. Most importantly, if you are unsure of something, ask an Israeli friend. We continue to do so when we are stumped and we probably will remain "stumped" for the rest of our lives.

General Living Costs

We have seen quite a number of social media posts asking about living costs prior to making aliya. It is more than reasonable to create budgets and ensure that you can live within them. It is difficult for us to offer a full-blown family budget with expenses because it depends on your stage of life and where you live in the country. Living expenses for those in

Jerusalem or the center of the country will be high in relation to the country's periphery, defined as every place outside of Jerusalem or the Tel Aviv area. Even within cities, rents vary widely. Another factor is your stage of life. A lone soldier, *bat sherut*, or university student will have different expenditures than a family with children. The best we can do is lay out some expenses you will have. Some are recurring expenditures, and some are one-time expenses; we lay out some of the differences for single olim vs. families.

The sections below repeat key terms a number of times. If you can't find the key term in the margin, refer to earlier pages or to Appendix C, Glossary of Terms.

Lone Soldiers and Bnot Sherut

Some lone soldiers try to find an apartment and live together, sharing all the expenses. If you are adopted by a family or part of *Garin Tzabar*, these expenses aren't an issue. Most of the expenses below are not incurred by *bnot sherut* since the National Service *(Sherut Leumi)* provides an apartment and covers related costs.

Bnot sherut
National Service volunteers

A word about those who chose to live together and share an apartment. Effectively, this means that roommates split all the costs below. Logistically, this is not the easiest thing to do, and disagreements can arise over splitting an electric bill when one lone soldier spent 21 days on base while others were home more often and benefited from the air-conditioning. These are issues that have to be worked out, so be aware of them.

- **Rent:** You will receive a small stipend of about NIS 1300, and it won't go far. Renting together with others is likely the only way. *Bnot sherut* get apartments for free.

■ **Furniture and appliances**: As noted more fully in Chapter 5, any apartment rented will lack basic amenities like closets, a stovetop, an oven, a washing machine, a dryer, and a refrigerator. It also won't have beds, tables, sofas, TVs, or dishes. Lone soldiers can receive quite a bit of donated used items but not everything. You might decide to purchase an item and split the cost among roommates, although when the time comes to vacate that apartment, there is always a discussion about who has ownership. *Bnot sherut* apartments will have the most basic amenities like a bed, a stovetop, and perhaps a washing machine but not much else. You will need to purchase or find a donation for dishes, toaster ovens, microwaves, and other items.

■ **Food**: Some lone soldier groups or communities offer you food for free, particularly on Shabbat, or you can eat with an adopted family. Be prepared to pay for groceries if neither comes through. Otherwise, most of a lone soldier's meals are on base. *Bnot sherut* get a small stipend for food, and they will be required to cook for themselves in their apartment. For Shabbat, they can eat with an adopted family or receive packages from some of the lone soldier groups that offer them. If neither comes through, *bnot sherut* will have to cook for themselves for Shabbat.

■ **Internet**: In Israel, you pay for the *tashtit* and separately for the *sapak*. A bill comes once a month. Lone soldiers who rent apartments together will have to pay for this. Mark your calendar as to when your contract is up; otherwise, the cost will automatically rise. *Bnot sherut* apartments may or may not come with Internet paid for by *Sherut Leumi*.

Tashtit
Infrastructure—in this case, for your Internet line (like a modem connection and the cables)

Sapak
Supplier, in this case, the company that provides your Internet service

■ **Television**: Cable packages cost money, as does the device itself. There used to be a time when you would pay a television tax even if you didn't have one. That is no longer the case. More and more young people seem to forgo televisions and access shows via the Internet.

■ **Electricity**: This is probably the highest recurring bill, and it comes every two months. Don't forget to turn off your AC when you leave for the base, or you will be hit with a big bill. If you have a dryer, it is likely to run on electricity, which can be expensive. It is unlikely that you have underfloor heating but if you do, it is a huge cost to run it, so don't flip the switch by accident. Know where the meter to your apartment is located. *Bnot sherut* electricity bills are covered by *Sherut Leumi*. And know how to flip the fuses back to the upward position when they blow.

Va'ad bayit
*Residents'
committee
and the
monthly
fees that
go towards
communal
upkeep of the
building*

■ **Va'ad bayit**: For the common areas of your building to be clean, every apartment in the complex pays a fee once a month. This is an expense incurred by lone soldiers sharing an apartment but not by *bnot sherut*.

Arnona
*Local prop-
erty taxes
paid to the
municipality.
Olim receive
a 90%
discount for
the first year
after aliya*

■ **Arnona**: You can pay municipal property taxes either in full or in monthly payments. This applies to lone soldiers, who receive *arnona* discounts and who rent an apartment together. There is no *arnona* cost for *bnot sherut*, since the apartments are paid for by *Sherut Leumi*.

■ **Water**: You pay for water use in your own apartment and in the common areas. The bill comes every two months. This expense is applicable to lone soldiers who rent an apartment together but not *bnot sherut*. Know where the meter to your apartment is located because you might need to know how to shut off the water if there is a leak.

- **Third-party insurance**: Some landlords want you to get third-party insurance for your apartment just in case something happens in the apartment.

- **Gas**: Not every apartment has a gas line, but if it does, the bill is a small one and comes every two months.

- **Heating and hot water**: Some apartments have a *yunkers*, a gas heating system. It is cheaper than running the air-conditioning for heat, which, in any event, is hardly effective. Regarding hot water, there is a *dood shemesh* on the roof of your building, which is a solar heating system for water. It should provide more than enough hot water in the summer months, but in some apartments even the solar system doesn't provide enough hot water and you find yourself turning on the electric *dood* when you need hot water. That is a large expense and one you will pay, particularly in the winter months. Don't forget to turn the electric *dood* off, and if you find yourself forgetting, put it on a timer (like we did).

  Yunkers
  Gas heating system

  _____

  Dood shemesh
  Solar heating system for water on the roof of a building

- **Cell phone plans**: The phone itself is a one-time cost that you pay out over the course of the contract. Most cell phone companies offer very good rates for lone soldiers and *bnot sherut*.

- **Public transportation, health insurance**: Free.

- **Leisure**: Discounts for soldiers, sometimes for *bnot sherut*, but you will still have to pay something.

University Students

There are dormitory buildings available for students, but some universities or colleges have rules about who can have them. Normally, dorms are reserved for students whose families live far away from the campus—i.e., in another city. Perhaps because of their age, most university students prefer to rent apartments together with other students rather than live in the dormitory. The list below does not include those who have cars, which is an entirely different expense as noted more fully later in this chapter.

- **Rent**: Depending on where you live, how big your apartment is, and how many roommates you have, this can be a cost of NIS 1,000-2,000 a month or even more.

- **Furniture and appliances**: If you received free items as a lone soldier, that won't be happening now. As noted more fully in Chapter 5, any apartment rented will lack basic amenities like closets, a stovetop, an oven, a washing machine, a dryer, and a refrigerator. It also won't have beds, tables, sofas, TVs, dishes, or microwaves. Look on Facebook groups for used items at a lower cost. If you and your roommates decide to purchase an item and split the cost, remember that when you vacate that apartment, there is always a discussion about who has ownership, and one roommate might have to "buy out" the others.

- **Food**: If you were a lone soldier, you probably received free food fairly often. That comes to an end in university. Food costs in Israel, even for standard products, are around 20%[3] more than in other OECD countries. Stay with "in-season" fruits and vegetables; otherwise, the expense rises.

- **Health insurance**: If you were in the army, you got used to mediocre albeit free medical care. Now you have to join a *kupa* and pay a small fee every month for that *kupa*.

- *Arnona:* These are municipal property taxes you pay either in full or monthly. University students must apply for a discount at the local municipal office.

Kupa
Health Insurance Plan

- **Public transportation:** What was free while you were a soldier or a *bat sherut* is now no longer free. You will likely have to get a monthly bus pass. Trains are a different system and have different costs. If you use a combination of the train and bus systems often, look into passes for both.

- **Cell phone plans**: What was cheaper for you as a lone soldier or *bat sherut* is now more expensive. The phone itself is a one-time cost that you pay out over the course of the contract. Mark your calendar as to when the contract ends or your monthly charges will automatically go up.

- **Leisure:** There are discounts for students but not for everything, and you will likely have to pay for something.

- **Internet, electricity, *va'ad bayit*, water, third-party insurance, gas, heating, and hot water:** The costs are the same as noted for lone soldiers and *bnot sherut*.

Young Couples or Families

Expenditures for families can vary with the number of children and, of course, the size of the apartment or the location. We tried our best to outline some of the expenses to expect:

- **Rent**: This varies based on the size of the apartment and the location. If you are a young family, don't underestimate the need for an apartment with outdoor space. Apartments are small, and when you have children, a small *mirpeset* or a small garden makes a big difference. If outdoor space isn't possible, try to find an apartment that is close to a community garden. Every neighborhood has one, and many have more than one, with nice play equipment. As soon as your children are legally allowed to walk around by themselves (age 9), you will want to be close to a community garden so that they can walk there on their own.

Mirpeset
Porch

- **Furniture and appliances**: We assume that you might want to live at a standard that is a notch or two higher than lone soldiers, *bnot sherut,* or university students. Accordingly, assume that you will have to purchase new or secondhand everything—like closets, a stovetop, an oven, a washing machine, a dryer, a refrigerator, beds, tables, sofas, and dishes. Measure every single space to make sure things fit and that you have sufficient electricity to run your devices. Whether you buy new or used will largely depend on your budget and on whether you have a long-term lease. For example, if you are renting an apartment for three years, purchasing something new can be economical. If you are in your apartment for a year, secondhand might be best even if it doesn't fit perfectly in the space.

- **Air-conditioning**: If your apartment doesn't have it, or if your apartment is wired for it but the former tenants took it with them, you will have a one-time cost of purchasing a new unit and hooking it up. Running it is an electrical cost as noted below.

- **Food**: As noted above, food costs are around 20% higher than in other OECD countries. Different chain stores have different prices, and sometimes your fruits and vegetables will be cheaper in one place and your dry goods will be cheaper in another. It makes shopping a bit of a hassle.

- **Internet**: In Israel, you pay for the *tashtit* and separately for the *sapak*. The bill comes once a month. Despite the fact that we are the Start Up Nation, service can be spotty. Ask your neighbors what company they use because they probably figured out what works best in your area. Mark your calendar as to when your contract is up because otherwise the cost will automatically rise.

- **Cell phone plans**: The phone itself is a one-time cost that you pay out over the course of the contract. Even if you have young children, you will have to buy a phone for them sooner than you thought. Look for family plans that suit the number of lines you have. Mark your calendar as to when the contract ends or your monthly charges will automatically go up.

- **Television**: Cable packages cost money, as does the device itself. There used to be a time when you paid a television tax even if you didn't have one. That is no longer the case. You might want to forgo cable in exchange for a large screen with streaming service.

■ **Electricity**: This is probably the highest recurring bill; it comes every two months. The air-conditioner and the electric dryer likely eat up a lot of the electricity bill. If you have underfloor heating, it is a wonderful thing, especially for young children who are still crawling, but it is a huge cost to run. Know where the meter to your apartment is located. And know how to flip the fuses back to the upward position when they blow.

■ *Va'ad bayit:* For the common areas of your building to be clean, every apartment in the complex pays a fee once a month.

■ *Arnona:* All olim get a 90% discount on their first year of *arnona*, and you must request it at the municipal offices. You can pay at once or make payments every month. The cost of your *arnona* will be determined by the size of your apartment, and it increases exponentially with your apartment or home size.

■ **Water**: If you live in an apartment complex, you pay for water use in your own apartment and in the common areas. If you live in your own home, there probably are no common area water costs, but it depends on where you live. The bill comes every two months. Know where the meter is located because you might need to know how to shut off the water.

■ **Home insurance**: If you own your home or apartment, you will need to insure the home and its contents from damage. Most home insurance policies will not cover beyond a certain amount of jewelry or other high-ticket items in your home, which means you need to pay for a safety deposit box separately. You will also not receive home insurance coverage without an alarm system or without bars on your windows, both of which are ostensibly to increase protection from theft.

■ **Alarm**: Installation is one time only, but you usually pay a monthly cost for the call center that monitors your alarm.

■ **Car insurance and gas**: See the end of this chapter for information about car insurance. The cost of owning one car is high enough. Owning two is prohibitive.

■ **Gas**: Not every apartment has a gas line. You might want to install one if possible, if nothing else than because gas is cheaper than electric. Installation will be a one-time fee; thereafter, the bill is a small one and comes every two months. We installed a special gas line for a gas dryer. Both were large expenses, but we undoubtedly saved on electric costs because the gas dryer is faster and cheaper to run.

■ **Heating and hot water**: Some apartments have a *yunkers*, a gas heating system. It is cheaper than running the air-conditioning for heat, which in any event is hardly effective. Regarding hot water, there is a *dood shemesh* on the roof of your building, a solar heating system for water. If you own your apartment and your *dood* bursts (which it can after a dramatic freeze/thaw cycle), you will have to replace it, which is a large expense. The *dood* system should provide more than enough hot water in the summer months, but in some apartments even the solar system doesn't provide enough hot water and you find yourself turning on the electric *dood* when you need hot water. That is a large expense and one you will pay, particularly in the winter months. If you have young children, install a timer on the *dood* so it heats up water before bath/shower time and turns off after. Otherwise, your children will quickly learn how to turn on the hot water but will forget to turn it off.

- **Public transportation:** If you are working, a monthly bus pass will be provided. If you have to take the bus and train systems, they have different costs; look for the best deal based on your travel needs.

- **Health insurance, public system:** The cost of the basic public health care system comes out of your salary as noted more fully below. We recommend that you buy "wrap around" additional policies that each *kupa* has, which gives you the ability to have certain "richer" health benefits. The cost will vary depending on your age and the ages of your children, and it is a monthly expense that will be charged to your credit card if you sign up for it.

- **Health insurance, private system:** It is worth investing in private insurance policies as additional coverage. Clearly, the younger you are, the cheaper they will be.

- **Day care:** For babies through kindergarten, there are *me'onot*, which will be a cost factor. In 2019, the OECD reported that Israel has the most expensive preschool in the entire OECD.[4]

Me'onot
Day care centers

- **Education:** The cost of education is largely approved by the Ministry of Education, and while it isn't much, it is a cost, and sometimes a relatively high one compared to salaries. It can range from NIS 7,000-15,000 annually for high school (and sometimes more, depending on the school) to NIS 3,400 annually (or more) for elementary school. This does not include other expenses like gifts for teachers, presents for children on different holidays, trips, year-end parties, and more. Although tuition costs might not appear to be expensive compared to your home country, note that in the past decade, elementary school costs rose 17% and junior high and high school costs went up by about 10%.[5]

■ **Summer camp and informal after-school** *chugim:* The cost of summer camp varies, but it can run in the thousands for a one-month program. Most of the summer camps run on a two-week basis, for a maximum of six weeks, leaving every parent scrambling during the last weeks of August. Informal education and summer camp rose by 13% in the past decade.[6]

■ **Books**: School books can be an expense if your school doesn't recycle books. You will receive a list of school books to purchase before the school year. You can and should buy used books if possible. The review books for the *bagrut* exams are quite costly.

■ **Clothes**: The good news is that the winter in Israel is generally short and winter gear, while needed in some areas, is not the same expense as those who live in colder climates that last longer. There are cheaper places and more expensive places. To purchase clothing, you will have to shop around.

■ **Leisure:** It is a well-known and unfortunate fact that taking a one-week vacation in Israel is more expensive than flying to Europe and renting a villa for a week. For reasons that are hard to fathom, even *tzimerim,* quaint cabins throughout the country, are very expensive. Perhaps for this reason, camping is common and fun; invest in good camping gear.

Tzimerim
Quaint cabins

The price of a movie is probably comparable to other countries, and streaming options that allow for in-home entertainment are nice family activities and can turn out to be cheaper than taking a whole family to the movies. Going out for a nice dinner is an expense because of the high cost of food and is reserved for special occasions, although if you have room for a *mangal*, a barbecue, it makes for a good time for the entire family.

Bank Accounts and Credit Cards

When you arrive in Israel, one of the first things to do is open a bank account. *Misrad HaKlita* will ask for it right away because your *sal klita* will be wired directly to your account. You will need your *teudat oleh*, your passport, and your *teudat zehut* to open a bank account. All American citizens are required to complete a W9 form as well as FACTA, an international banking disclosure requirement. We generally advise opening up an account that is closest to your home because you might find yourself wanting to meet with a bank teller, and those are increasingly rare thanks to online banking, which is done primarily in Hebrew.

Amalot, bank charges (i.e., transaction costs), are an enigma even to most Israelis, and to try and understand or fight these charges can be maddening. Laws governing banks can change, and some of us have just stopped trying to understand it all, chalking it up to the cost of living in Israel.

There are three basic numbers every oleh should know: *mispar bank, snif*, and *mispar heshbon*. These are crucial for nearly all bank transactions. All banks have very good mobile applications to monitor your bank account, transfer/wire

Mangal
Barbecue: noun and verb

Misrad HaKlita
Ministry of Absorption and Immigration

Sal klita
Absorption basket, a fixed sum of money for a six-month period

Teudat oleh
A booklet that reflects your aliya date to track your rights

Teudat zehut
Blue identity card that you are required by law to carry with you at all times

Amalot
Fees and charges

Mispar bank
Bank number: all banks have numbers, then branch numbers, then your bank account number

money, and otherwise conduct a large number of online banking transactions. The English apps are usually a "light" version of the Hebrew, but many operational transactions like a bank transfer or foreign exchange are not always doable on the bank's English site. The English site is better for review of information but not for banking activity. It is therefore best to learn certain banking terms that come up again and again in Israeli life, such as *kaspomat, hafkada, ha'avra bankait, m'zuman, pinkas shek, m'shicha, hamra'a matach,* and *hora'at keva.* There are many more terms worth knowing, but this is a good start.

Hora'at keva is a very common phenomenon. It might seem like a monthly credit charge, but it is not. When you have a recurring monthly charge—for example, your cell phone, home Internet, or even school tuition—you might be sent a *hora'at keva* to complete. It is a standard one-page form. You fill in your bank account information and get your bank to stamp the form. Once it is approved by the bank, the *hora'at keva* authorizes an institution to automatically draw a set amount of money from your bank account on a certain date in the month. Once a *hora'at keva* is in effect, you have to go to the bank in person to cancel it. If at all possible, it is better to use your credit card to charge expenses inasmuch as it is easier to cancel a credit card charge than it is to cancel a *hora'at keva.*

Banks automatically allow you to have a certain monthly overdraft known as *minus.* This is quite a frightening statement for many who did not know it in advance or for parents to whom this will be a completely foreign and dangerous concept. The difficulty in carrying monthly costs against your salary is the motivation behind overdraft allowances for up to a certain amount. The Central Bureau of Statistics reports that 42% of families in 2018 were in

Snif
Prounounced "sneef": Bank branch number, generally your local bank

Mispar heshbon
Bank account number

Kaspomat
ATM

Hafkada
Deposit

Ha'avra bankait
Wire transfer

M'zuman
Cash

Pinkas shek
Checkbook

M'shicha
Bank withdrawal

Hamra'a matach
Exchange of foreign currency (matach stands for matbe'a chutz)

Hora'at keva
Standing order to withdraw money on a monthly basis

overdraft at least one month in the previous year. Half of them reported that this is their "general situation" and that they were in overdraft 10 months in the past year.[7] Although online banking has improved drastically over the years, a command of Hebrew will be necessary to use them.

Kartisei ashra'i, credit cards, are really debit cards and are connected to your bank account. There are certain limits placed on the amount that can be charged to that credit card monthly, and it is generally tied to your salary. It is not that difficult to increase your "credit line" so that you can charge more per month. You are frequently offered the opportunity to charge a purchase in *tashlumim,* which essentially means spreading a charge over a number of months. Every Israeli does it, but this does not mean it is a smart thing to do. If you use *tashlumim,* you spread out the payment of a purchase for a long period of time. This means you really never have a handle on your credit card bill in any given month, unless you are constantly looking at your credit card statement. Try as best you can to budget yourself and avoid too many *tashlumim.*

Employment-Related Finances and Documents

If you landed your first job in Israel, congratulations! You are now a *sachir,* and you get to learn all about Israel's work culture up close. There are some terms and documents you will encounter in the course of your Israeli employment.

An employment contract is known as a *chozeh,* the same word used for any contract. It is an important document, and it is nearly always in Hebrew. It doesn't necessarily have to be long, but it should lay out, at a bare minimum, your *bruto maskoret,* what kind of *misrah* it is (full-time or part-time job), hours per week or month, minimum vacation time under the law, minimum sick

---

Kartis ashra'i
Credit card

Tashlumim
Payment plan to spread out payments for a given purchase, normally without "rib-it," interest

---

Sachir
Salaried employee

Chozeh
Contract, in this case, an employment contract

Bruto maskoret
Gross salary: your net

Misrah
Job position or posting

time under the law, pension, and other deductions as required. Don't sign it if you don't understand it. Get someone to help you read through it before you commit to it.

No one in Israel refers to their salary as annual. Our salaries are monthly, reflected in gross pay, and in NIS. It's not advisable to evaluate your NIS salary in your former currency simply because it isn't a transferable figure. Once you decide to live in Israel, you live in shekels. Your bills are in shekels and your income is in shekels.

Tofes 101, a *kartis oved*, is the first employment-related form you will be asked to sign. It is a standard double-sided form in which you fill in your personal information, the names and *teudat zehut* numbers of your children, your marital status, and whether you hold any other job. More on this later.

The second side of the *Tofes 101* includes many boxes to be reviewed and checked off if relevant. These boxes are crucial for your *nekudot zikui*, tax credit points, which make a significant difference in your net pay. As an *oleh*, you must check the box that you are an oleh hadash. If you completed the IDF or National Service, you must check this box as well and attach documents that demonstrate you completed your service. Failure to check these boxes means you will not receive the tax credits you deserve, and it will impact your net pay. Your salary will be paid directly into your bank account; to make this happen, you will have to give your employer precise banking information.

By law, you will receive your salary into your bank by the 10th of every month. By law, you are entitled to something called a *chofshi chodshi*, a bus pass that covers public transportation, although on occasion your employer might also reimburse you for gas or other transportation expenses. By law, you are entitled to a *t'lush maskoret*, a pay stub that includes your gross salary, tax credits, and deductions, which include *Bituach Leumi*, pension, and other items noted below. Review your pay stubs, make sure

---

Tofes 101
Kartis oved: Worker's card, a form completed by every employee annually

Nekudot zikui
Tax credits that apply to olim, single parents, those who served in the IDF/National Service, and others

Chofshi chodshi
Monthly bus pass reflected in your salary

T'lush maskoret
Israeli pay stub

Bituach Leumi
Behemoth government institution that manages the entire social welfare net for the country

Kupat holim
Socialized national health insurance

Bituach briyut
Health insurance— in this case, reflected in your pay stub as a deduction to cover the socialized medical system

Pensia, kupot gemel, and bituach minhalim
Terms related to private pension fund deductions that are required by law

Pitzuim
Severance pay

Atzma'i
Independent contractor or freelancer

you understand them, and save every one of them because you might need them down the road.

As an oleh, you have some income tax breaks for a period of time, but they do expire. You receive three tax credit points during your first 18 months after aliya, two points for the year thereafter, and one point in the third year. Thereafter, you are taxed at the "regular" Israeli income tax rates. Income tax rates are levied based on the individual's income and not on joint income earned by a married couple. The tax bands are based on your annual salary and currently start at 10% for up to NIS 75,000 annual salary and rise to 14% (NIS 108,000), 20% (NIS 175,000), 31% (NIS 243,000), 35% (NIS 505,000), 47% (NIS 651,000), and 50% (above NIS 651,000).

Bituach Leumi, the National Insurance Institute, is the umbrella government institution responsible for a wide array of social welfare benefits ranging from unemployment to disability, retirement pay, and child and elderly allowances. It's a behemoth of an organization, and every employee and employer pays into it to cover Israel's extensive social welfare net. An employee pays 5% into *Bituach Leumi*. Most people assume that health care *(kupat holim)* is free, but you will find that your pay stub includes a 5% deduction to cover *bituach briyut*, effectively your contribution to the socialized health care system.

There was a time when the state assumed that *Bituach Leumi* would cover living expenses for retirees. With life expectancy on the rise, the State of Israel passed laws that require every person to contribute to a private pension fund in addition to their *Bituach Leumi*. The relevant terms you need to know here are *pensia, kupot gemel,* and *bituach minhalim*. An employer contributes 6.5% of the salary and the employee contributes 6% (these numbers can change). All workers are entitled to *pitzuim*, severance pay. The employer contributes 8.3% of the base salary, which is paid to a laid-off employee or sometimes to one who resigns. It is important to know that pension is required by law even if you are a freelancer, an *atzma'i*, an independent contractor, and you are also required to pay *Bituach Leumi*. See the section below on opening up a business.

Pension issues are complicated for most olim because they don't necessarily correspond to the pension plans olim might have had before aliya. Our best advice is to find an insurance agent and not just rely on your employer's human resource personnel or the pension fund company it uses. Your own agent will look out for your interests and your needs, advising what is best for your stage in life.

After one year, employees are entitled under the law to *d'mei havra'a,* convalescence pay, designed to help employees take vacation. The payment is made either in the summer months or in 12 monthly payments.

Keren hishtalmut is an optional benefit that not everyone receives but is a nice benefit to have. The employee contributes 2.5% of the employee's salary and the employer contributes 5% or 7.5%. The funds are "locked up" and are not liquid until year seven for the employee's use.

Finally, there are situations where Israelis have more than one job, say two part-time jobs, one at 60% time and one at 40% time, or even 50/50. In these circumstances, to ensure you are not double taxed, you will need to record your other job information on the *Tofes 101* and you will need to do a *te'um mas,* a coordination of income, with *Mas Hachnasa* (the Income Tax Authority) so that the employers know how much income tax to withhold. These are complicated issues, and it is worth looking up information on a variety of Hebrew websites.

D'mei havra'a
Convalescence pay, which is designed to help employees take vacation and is generally paid in the summer months

---

Keren hishtalmut
Optional benefit in which employee contributes 2.5% of salary and employer contributes 5 or 7.5%

Te'um mas
Coordination of income so that you don't pay double tax when you hold more than one job

---

Mas Hachnasa
Israel's Income Tax Authority

Osek patur
Small business for which value-added tax is waived under a certain income amount

---

Osek mursheh
Small business that otherwise operates as a regular business above a certain income amount

---

Ma'am
Mas erech musaf: VAT

Tik
Pronounced "teek." File that you open in any government office

Opening Up a Business

If you have chosen to open up a business of any kind, even a service-related consulting business, you have the option of opening up an *osek patur* or an *osek mursheh*. Understand that either one of these raises complicated tax issues, and we recommend you consider finding an accountant to help with the paperwork.

An *osek patur* means a business for which *ma'am* (*mas erech mosaf, VAT*) is waived because it is not expected to earn enough income. To qualify as an *osek patur*, you estimate that you will not earn more than NIS 100,000 per year, but be aware that this number can change annually. The catch is that certain professions are excluded from being an *osek patur*. The Israeli Tax Authority publicizes a list; as of this writing, a business consultant or a writer cannot be an *osek patur*. You must open a *tik* in *Mas Hachnasa* and with *Bituach Leumi*, for you will be paying taxes every quarter directly to them based on estimated income. You can always upgrade to an *osek morsheh* if you earn income above the *osek patur* limit. Be aware that you can go above the limit fast, and you can be taxed retroactively for the income you earned prior to NIS 100,000. Once you are an *osek mursheh*, you will have to charge VAT on your bill to others and refer that money back to the government.

The steps to opening up an *osek patur* are not complicated, and upgrading to an *osek mursheh* might also not be difficult. However, you can experience accountancy problems, so we advise you to consult with professionals before you go down the freelancer road. Remember that either of these independent contractor categories means that you do not get paid vacation or sick leave. For you, it is just a day that you don't get paid. Also keep in mind that even an *osek patur* is required to pay income tax, and both businesses must pay *Bituach Leumi* and pension. Failure to do any of these in a timely manner can mean fines, an attempt to take money from your private checking account, and a whole host of other challenges that you'd rather not face.

If a company offers to pay you as an independent contractor or a freelancer, it is likely that it doesn't want to incur the social welfare expenses that are so high for Israeli employers. A company that wants to employ you as a freelancer will ask you to issue bills and receipts, all while having you deal with the entire tax and social welfare system on your own. You are certainly free to make that choice, but be aware of the consequences ranging from a significant amount of your own paperwork to lack of a social welfare net. It might look like you earn more money as an independent contractor, but it can be a fallacy. You might prefer being employed as a salaried employee, albeit at a lower income level, just to avoid the bureaucratic obstacle course.

It is for these reasons that if you decide to open a business, we highly recommend that you scour the Internet, do your research, find professionals who have done this before, and get help through the process—if nothing else than to save you from a headache down the road.

Apartments and Related Expenses

Over the years, the logistics behind apartment hunting have gotten easier thanks to social media groups. Most young olim will likely rent an apartment together or will join an apartment that already has other roommates. The older the olim, the more likely they will rent their own apartment.

Apartments in Israel often lack some basic appliances that would otherwise be part of a rental in other parts of the world, like ovens, refrigerators, stovetops, washing machines, dryers, and air-conditioners. If tenants purchase these items, they can take them when they move. This includes bed frames, mattresses, closets, desks, tables, and other items as well. Although appliances and other household items are generally not prohibitively expensive, young olim tend to skimp on what they perceive as conveniences to save on costs, like foregoing a standard oven in exchange for a toaster oven or a dryer in exchange for the sun. It is understandable that young people tend to make do with very little; however, you can circumvent austere and spartan living arrangements by joining Facebook groups and Facebook Marketplace to buy used items at reasonable prices.

Certain household appliances might not be expensive to purchase but can be expensive to run. For example, most dryers in Israel are electric and are not particularly expensive. However, electric costs in Israel are high, and the electric bill (sent every two months) is often the most expensive household utility (after local property taxes known as *arnona*). Running an electric dryer is expensive, but the purchase of it is less so. Gas dryers are available, but they are expensive to purchase, and most apartments need a special gas line installed to run them. Air-conditioning units are also expensive to run, but considering the length of the summer, you might simply purchase one and take it with you when you move.

Apartment leases were the subject of regulatory reform a few years ago. For a long period of time, apartment owners increased rents at unreasonable rates (because they could), failed to offer certain basic amenities like a working bathroom (because they could), refused to make reasonable repairs (because they could), and demanded high-priced security deposits or guarantees (because they could). Although the law has changed, we have seen more than our fair share of contracts that we would not necessarily agree to and, in some cases, we were able to secure more reasonable conditions when we had an opportunity to see leases before they were signed.

Nearly all olim will encounter a landlord who will want the tenants to find an *arev*, someone who guarantees to honor the terms of the lease if the tenant does not. Most landlords will not accept a guarantor who isn't Israeli. We have been guarantors for a few olim, and we largely felt comfortable doing so because we knew the overseas parents stood by their children and would honor their children's commitments. The agreement to become a guarantor is a highly personal one, and if you have friends in Israel, they will come in handy as a guarantor.

All rental contracts require some sort of *pikadon*, a security deposit to cover damage to the apartment that might be discovered after the lease is up. The law today does not allow any more than three months' rent for this security deposit. The landlord might also ask for *hafkadat check patuach*, open checks to the water, gas, and electric companies, should you finish the lease without paying the final utility bills. Make sure that all contracts include provisions for returning the security deposit and the open utility checks when the lease is over.

Regarding utility bills and other related household expenditures, you generally receive the water, electric, and gas bills every two months. You can either give these utilities your credit card to get charged every month or you can choose to pay the bill on receipt. Doing the latter ensures your control, and it is very easy to do either online or even via telephone. You will receive an *asmachta* number, which is essentially a receipt number that you should write down on the bill, in addition to the date that you paid it.

Arev
Guarantor

Pikadon
Deposit—in this case, some kind of security deposit to protect property

Hafkadat check patuach:
Open check that is signed—in this context, for utilities

Asmachta
Receipt or document number

Your Lift

Olim are entitled to ship a *lift* to Israel, which Israelis call a container. There is a common misconception that the lift is free. It is not. Shipping to Israel incurs costs, but as olim, much of what you import to the country will be free of customs tax. There are some exceptions, and there are some items that are simply not economical to ship, particularly if they require importing replacement parts or paying for service when there are no expert servicemen in Israel. It is possible that young olim will be able to bring their prized possessions without shipping on a lift.

Our personal recommendation is to ship as little as possible. Spaces in Israel are smaller, which means large living room furniture or beds might not fit, to say nothing of the bedding, which can be different measurements entirely. Fluffy couches that trap dust might not be what you want in Israel, a country with sand that creeps in all the time. Appliances, like very large washing machines and dryers, are wonderful to have because those sold in Israel are genuinely smaller and hold less. However, if you bring appliances from outside of Israel, you do it at your peril. Israel might not have technicians or parts to service the appliance when it needs repairing.

Cars are highly taxed in Israel, and we have heard of some families who decided to ship their car to Israel. We opted to purchase one here, using our aliya benefits (tax deductions) so that our car could more easily be serviced here.

Online Purchases

Many olim believe they can order items online and have them shipped to Israel, even small items that are easy to package and ship. For a short period of time, Amazon shipped to Israel for free for orders above $50 but, as of this writing, that deal is no longer available. Another important thing to know about is *meches,* the Israeli tax authority at points of entry that looks at every shipped package. If you ship more than $75 worth of goods to Israel, you run the risk of *meches* holding the package and charging you VAT. You are at the mercy of *meches* if it decides not to allow the package in at all, for you will have paid for a product that you might never receive.

Finally, to family and friends who don't live in Israel, we are sorry that we occasionally, or very frequently, ask you to lug something when you come to visit. We have come a long way, and items like deodorant, tuna, aluminum foil, makeup, and sealable bags are available and even affordable. A lot can be shipped to Israel if we maintain purchases under $75. Any more than that can incur value-added tax at border control. Although we will ask for fewer favors than we used to, requests for family members to bring items to Israel might be an arrangement that can go on forever. We still do it.

Meches
Israeli tax authority, operating at ports of entry, to evaluate costs of shipped items and to decide whether tax should be added to the purchase

Car Insurance and Driver's License

In general, a car purchased in Israel is double what it would cost elsewhere because of the import tax. We know olim who shipped cars on their lift largely because the vehicle they wanted wasn't available in Israel (like a specific minivan). One way or the other, be aware of the purchase cost in Israel vs. the shipping cost.

Thanks to the lobbying work of Keep Olim, a law was passed that now allows new olim to convert their driver's licenses without taking new lessons. You can convert a foreign license within five years of aliya if you had five consecutive years

Bituach rechev
Car insurance

Rishayon rechev
Annual cost for your license plate

Bituach chova
Compulsory car insurance

Bituach makif
Comprehensive car insurance (but really both types are needed)

Nahag chadash
New driver up to the age of 24, for whom car insurance is quite expensive

Delek
Gasoline

of a valid driver's license for the immediate five-year period prior to making aliya.[8]

Once you pass your driving test and you have a car, you will have to purchase insurance called *bituach rechev.* First, there is the *rishayon rechev,* and while this literally translates as car license, it is not what it means. It means car registration, and there is a flat fee for the privilege of having license plates. You pay for that privilege with a *rishayon rechev.* The cost is dependent on the type of car your drive and how old it is.

Once a year, your car needs to be inspected, but you can't do that until you pay the *rishayon rechev.* Once you do, you go to a local car garage with the approved receipt from the *rishayon recehv* and get your car inspected. This annual inspection is called a *test.* Really, that is the actual word used. You need to have valid car insurance before the test is done, so try to time your test for the last month before your insurance lapses.

Car insurance includes two elements: *bituach chova* (compulsory) and *bituach makif* (comprehensive). *Bituach chova* covers legal requirements for car ownership. The cost is determined by the type of vehicle, age of drivers, accident history, car safety features, and usage. *Bituach chova* offers unlimited liability coverage for bodily injury to the driver, passengers, and pedestrians who may be involved in an accident. Each car covers its own passengers irrespective of who is at fault. Be aware that new drivers (i.e., teenagers who get a driver's license up through the age of 24) are considered a *nahag chadash,* and it costs quite a bit of money to insure them.

Bituach makif covers theft and accidents. It covers any damage to your vehicle and any third-party vehicle up to the sums specified in your car insurance policy. It also covers any depreciation on the market value of your car as a result of damage caused by an accident.

The price of gasoline *(delek)* in this country is high, double what it is in most other countries, which adds to the cost of car ownership. Most families cannot afford two cars, and if they have a second car, there is a high likelihood that one of the cars is an employer-provided benefit, with attenuating costs covered by the employer.

Israelis are notoriously aggressive drivers. Annually, more people are killed in car crashes than in war or terrorist incidents. Think about this. On Memorial Day 2020, Israel remembered our fallen soldiers and victims of terror, a total of 23,816 recorded since 1860.[9] By 2017, since the creation of the state in 1948, more than 33,352 Israelis were killed in car accidents, 40% more than all of our fallen war dead and terror victims tabulated in the past 160 years.[10]

13

And If All Else Fails

"Anyone who attempts isn't a failure."

—Sarah Dessen, Author[1]

"You can always come back" is a phrase many of us hear when we announce our aliya, when we are at the airport, or if we complain too often about Israeli life or Israelis themselves. Regardless of age, family and friends mean well when they remind us that aliya is reversible. It's great to have dreams, they say, but you can easily slip right back into an easier life. In the seven decades since Israel's birth, it is nearly impossible to quantify how many olim came to Israel with this "back-pocket option," but there were undoubtedly those who never had such an option to begin with.

Holocaust survivors who arrived during the pre-State British Mandate period and in the aftermath of the state's creation in 1948 hardly had a "home" to return to. The same could be said of the 850,000 Jews from Arab countries (Iran, Iraq, Morocco, Algeria, Tunisia, Yemen, Egypt, Syria, Lebanon, and Libya) who immigrated to Israel because they were exiled from their countries after the state's creation. Some might have managed to remain in their Arab homelands for a period, but the 1956 Suez crisis and the 1967 Six Day War all but finalized the exodus of virtually all remaining Jews from Arab countries.[2] Like Holocaust survivors, it is hard to imagine that they could easily "return home" if Israel did not work out for them.

Ethiopian immigration came in two large waves—in 1984 (Operation Moses) and in 1991 (Operation Solomon)—and Ethiopian Jews still immigrate to Israel today, although the vast majority are already here. And the most demonstrative immigration wave, at least in terms of pure numbers, was the nearly one million Jews from former Soviet Union (FSU) countries who immigrated after the fall of the Berlin Wall. Today, Jews continue to immigrate from the Ukraine, Russia, and other FSU bloc countries, but it is hard to know how many arrive with an escape hatch in mind.

Yes, olim leave Israel, but so do Israelis. In 2018, around

14,000 Israelis left Israel for a year or more.[3] The median age was 29, 52.8% of those who left were men, and around 50% who left did so with spouses. Of the Jewish population who left, 57.6% were born outside of Israel (olim) and 42.4% were born in Israel. "Sabras," native Israelis, as noted more fully below, feel the limited economic opportunity here, as evidenced by yet another statistic. According to the United States Department of Homeland Security, 87,000 Israelis received American citizenship or green card status between 2006-2016, *after* the second intifada ended and during a period of relative economic prosperity in Israel.[4] Once people emigrate from Israel (also known as *yerida,* descending from Israel as opposed to aliya, "rising up" to Israel), no one tracks where they take up residence. Olim, for example, can return to their country of origin, as was the case with the recent wave of immigrants from France, or they can end up in the United States, having originated more than 20 years earlier from the FSU.

Yerida
Leaving
Israel

It hardly matters where Israelis end up after they leave. The reasons they leave are of greater interest, particularly when they correlate to the reasons olim leave. Some Israelis leave for a year; others leave for good. In more recent years, Israelis left Israel for financial reasons, relocated to join an Israeli company scaling outside of Israel, or left because the cost of living held back their advancement. Unfortunately, it is the most educated and most-highly trained who leave because they can be better compensated abroad.[5] Other factors are also at play. Home acquisition is a huge burden, with the ratio of home prices to average income being one of the highest in the world. Household final consumption prices are 28% higher than in the United States, and the wage gap between Americans with undergraduate degrees is 95% higher.[6]

The Israeli press rightfully characterizes the emigration from Israel as a "brain drain," with the best and brightest

Israelis leaving the country to pursue opportunities unavailable to them in Israel. As of 2013, one out of every nine Israelis granted Ph.D.s left Israel, and in 2016, 14% of Israeli-trained doctors worked in other OECD countries.[7] All told, according to the Central Bureau of Statistics, somewhere between 563,000 and 600,000 Israeli citizens lived outside of Israel at the end of 2018,[8] although we have seen reports as far back as 2011 indicating that the numbers stood at 750,000 to one million.[9]

This shows that Israelis leave too. You can't fault olim for leaving when true "sabras"—born, educated, and raised in Israel—leave the country also. Simply put, Israel is a hard place to live, and people—olim *and* native Israelis—look for better opportunities elsewhere.

How many olim leave, and when do they decide to pull up stakes? Of the olim who left Israel in 2018, 67.6% made aliya between 2008 and 2018. Of those who left in 2018, 11% had aliya dates between 2008 and 2013, and 56.4% made aliya within the previous five years (2014-2018). These numbers tend to show that olim do indeed leave, and of those who left in 2018, the data suggests that many more left *within five years.* If you manage to stay between five and 10 years after your aliya, the chances of your leaving decrease, at least based on the 2018 figures.

It is important to note that there are no ongoing statistics, database, or research that explains specifically *why* olim leave when they do, nor does the available data distinguish between the motivations of olim who leave vs. the Israeli-born. Overall, the Central Bureau of Statistics notes that among all those who leave the country, 37.4% of them are between the ages of 20 and 40, evidencing their emigration for academic or work reasons. Regarding olim specifically, Nefesh B'Nefesh's website reports a variety of North American retention rates over the years, all at 90% or above. The 2018 Central Bureau of Statistics indicate that among those who left Israel in 2018, 71.7% originated from Europe, 20% from America and the Oceanic, 4.8% from Asia, and 3.5% from Africa. French aliya saw an uptick in 2015, with 8,000 French Jews who arrived in 2015 alone, but the number quickly dwindled to a third of that by 2018. According to Qualita, an organization for French immigrants, 10% of French olim return to France within three years of their aliya.[10]

In the absence of statistical references that explain why olim leave when they do, we relied on press reports that anecdotally reflect the main reasons for their decisions to leave.[11] Olim of any age are willing to talk publicly about their reasons for leaving Israel. There is even a Facebook group called Leaving Israel-The Official *Yerida* Group For People Who Want To GTFO. In a Facebook Group called "Secret Jerusalem," Sammy Katz, an oleh from the United States, posted a simple question: "In your opinion, what are the biggest reasons that (new) olim leave Israel?" In less than 24 hours, it elicited hundreds of comments. The 560-plus comments on Katz's post reflect the high level of engagement and interest in the thread's topic. We reduced the comments to around 200 that have explicit reasons for leaving Israel. Of those 200, 84 indicated, in one way or another, that decisions to leave are financial—cost of living, inability to support basic needs, lack of gainful employment, no opportunity for advancement, small business failures, difficulty in home ownership, and financial ease elsewhere. Forty-four comments fell into the "cultural" divide category, citing inability to adapt, difficulty with an aggressive society, rudeness, feelings of inadequacy or being put down, corruption, or the need to fight too hard. Thirty-six comments mentioned unreasonable expectations, including poor advance planning, false ideology, being "sold a bill of goods," or running away from problems that followed them to Israel. The remainder cited distance from family (14), language (12), and education (8). We would caution that our conclusions based on one Facebook thread are not statistical and only reflect commenters' passion for the issue.

Of all press reports and social media posts that we reviewed, the following were the most common reasons we found for leaving Israel:

- **Financial:** For these purposes, financial difficulties can mean employment, inability to support oneself on one's salary, high cost of living, lack of affordable housing, inability to advance, unable to succeed in a small business, and easier to financially manage elsewhere. Finding a job that supports the high cost of living is challenging. Even when olim find decent-paying jobs, they are often underemployed, they have a limited career path, their stellar educational bona fides are not valued in Israel, or they hit a glass ceiling with little advancement opportunity.

- **Language, Culture, Community, and Contention:** Many olim arrive in Israel knowing little or no Hebrew, and it is compounded by a lack of cultural understanding. They sign contracts they don't understand and encounter bureaucracy they can't manage, and it can lead to exploitation, which sours their experience. Olim have reported an inability to adapt to aggressiveness, rudeness, feelings of inadequacy, being taken advantage of, being put down as an immigrant and tiring of life being so hard all the time. The need to be proactive in nearly every aspect of life can be draining on many who didn't expect it.

- **Integration vs. Isolation/Loneliness:** Starting life anew means finding a community that was previously "built into" an oleh's former life. A few olim reported that Israelis were not welcoming and their status as olim was worse than being a Jew in their home country. Others simply found themselves missing the support system that comes from having a family nearby and not a plane flight away. Nefesh B'Nefesh contends that olim who settle in strong English-speaking communities were more likely to stay in Israel long term, as were married couples.

■ **Unreasonable Expectations**: There are those who admit that their planning was not adequate, they did not have reasonable expectations of how hard it would be, and there was too much emphasis on the positive elements of aliya without honestly addressing the challenges.

■ **Pensions**: For those who made aliya when they were older (like many from the former Soviet Union), they did not work long enough in the Israeli system, if at all, and Israeli pensions or the social welfare net failed to cover their expenses.

Unlike any other country, Israel has a national policy to promote and encourage immigrants. Overall, the country does a good job of keeping immigrants here. Contrary to past immigration waves, many of today's olim are not running away from persecution. Instead, they sacrifice a reasonably stable lifestyle, economic reliability, and culturally comfortable lives to move to Israel. Olim who stay in Israel can often tick off a list of friends who left for many of the reasons previously noted. One of the brave souls who stuck it out despite many hardships was LiAmi Lawrence. He can list nearly 350 friends who left and filled a void by creating a nonprofit called "Keep Olim." It offers a wide variety of services that can offset some of the cultural, employment, emotional, legal, and communal challenges. There are many others who personally reach out to olim to help them confront some of their absorption obstacles.

We asked olim and parents in our survey whether they knew of anyone who made aliya who left Israel within 5 years and if so, under what circumstances? A total of 113 respondents answered this open-ended question, as detailed more fully in Figure 1, which shows that 43% of those who left Israel did so for economic reasons.

Figure 1: Respondents who indicated that they know of olim who left Israel within 5 years of aliya, and the reasons for leaving

They know people who have left	Olim	Parents	Total
Yes	94	19	113

Reason for leaving	Olim	Parents	Total
Economic/ Financial	42	7	49
After IDF service	20	1	21
Nonintegration/culture	34	5	39
Distance from family	27	2	29
Security/danger	4	1	5

Our survey seems to confirm other anecdotal information that financial difficulty or economic hardship is one of the most common reasons for leaving Israel, followed by difficulty in acculturalization.

We note that the reports on *yerida* don't seem to mention the elephant in the room: leaving the country during wartime. Those of us who have endured countless rounds of violence in Israel might have developed a thicker skin, and in a short period of time we learned what it means to suffer through an awfully insecure time (weeks or months), only to find that when it ends, we bounce back to regular life fairly quickly. Resilience is part of an Israeli's DNA. It does not, however, stop worried parents overseas from suggesting that their children return to the "safe zone" of home, a place that has less geopolitical conflict. Conflict in the region was probably well known to olim before they came; it didn't seem to stop them and isn't likely to be a reason they leave. Parents watching our conflict play out on television screens might feel differently and want their children home, no matter what their age.

It is worth noting again here that more people in Israel are killed in car crashes than in war or terrorist incidents. On Memorial Day 2020, Israel remembered our fallen soldiers and victims of terror, a total of 23,816 recorded since 1860.[12] By 2017, since the creation of the state in 1948, more than 33,352 Israelis were killed in car accidents,[13] 40% more than all of our fallen war dead and terror victims tabulated in the past 160 years.

Our focus in this book has been on those who made aliya between the ages of 18 and 35. Olim in this age group who ultimately decide to leave Israel probably fall into two groups:

- **Group 1, Around Age 22, After IDF or National Service:** Those who leave after service in the IDF or National Service we characterize as civilian "societal entry" challenges. Even Israeli-born released soldiers have difficulty with civilian "reentry," but they "reenter" a society they know, which includes family; a home; a support system; and advice on how to navigate the next steps of their lives, including university and beyond. Olim in this age group, contrary to their Israeli-born counterparts, never lived in Israel as civilians. They entered mandatory service right after they made aliya, enjoyed special status as lone soldiers, received far more benefits than other soldiers, and must now chart their civilian course—largely alone. Their first entry into Israeli civilian life includes a range of complex decisions: where to live, which university and course of study is appropriate for them, entrance exams if need be, and a job to pay the rent. And they do it with no support system or close family. We know of one lone soldier who made aliya directly to the IDF as part of the Garin Tzabar program; according to him, of the 43 in his group, a majority returned.

- **Group 2, Ages 23-30:** Olim who make aliya after the mandatory draft age (22) might come with a university degree, some work experience, or a young family or might attempt university in Israel, itself an enormous challenge as we discussed in Chapter 8. Olim in this age group leave the country for many of the same reasons native Israelis do, with the significant exception of the language and cultural barriers. Cultural barriers can mean anything from language, dealing with Israeli bureaucracy, downright societal rudeness, or inability to land in a supportive community. Some of the anecdotal stories we uncovered include a 30-year-old who could not find employment since his aliya three years prior;

an educated 23-year-old married couple who left after a few years because their long and unfulfilling work hours did not cover their living expenses and because they did not find a suitable community; a 24-year-old journalist who came with an undergraduate and a graduate degree, only to return to her home country eight months later for financial reasons and because she disliked the aggressive culture; and a young couple who recently had a child and decided to leave Israel for financial reasons, for educational quality, and to be closer to grandparents.[14]

There is an as-yet unproven hypothesis that the younger you are when you make aliya, the easier your integration will be. Youth are generally not burdened with large-scale financial obligations, and it makes them more flexible. If you have young children, their absorption will undoubtedly be easier, for language acquisition is always smoother when you are younger. All olim are provided with intense language immersion programs *(ulpan);* they can more easily adjust to cultural changes; and to top it all off, they serve the country side-by-side with native Israelis. While there is no hard data that explains why Group 1 or Group 2 leaves Israel, if the hypothesis is correct, they ought to have succeeded because of their youth—they served like every other Israeli, they participated in *ulpan*, they came with an education or completed an education here, and they came willingly with a love for Israel that should have pulled them through rough times. It is hard to know if our hypothesis is flawed in the absence of data.

We assume that those who complete their service *and* university in Israel have a greater chance of "making it," but here too we lack data to support this theory. Policy makers should consider tracking these olim, and perhaps others who made aliya within the past 10 years, to better understand what made them stay in Israel when others left. The converse is also worth surveying—who left, when did they leave, and why—but here, it is important to focus on the differences between olim and native Israelis who leave. In our view, the financial motivation to emigrate is a common denominator for both groups. Other issues, like acculturalization and management of expectations, are unique to olim and are worthy of study if Israel wants to stem the tide and create a holistic set of programs that give olim a greater shot at staying.

In 2016, the 20th Knesset passed the *"Yom Ha'Aliyah"* law, officially adding it to the Israeli national calendar, and this not-so-wordy 14-line law[15] is intended to recognize the importance of Jewish immigration to Israel as a basis for the existence of the state and its development as a multicultural society. "Aliya Day" is annually recognized on the 7th of the Hebrew month of Heshvan, falling sometimes in late October or early November, and comes with a special session in the Knesset, events to honor olim at the President's residence, and IDF and school ceremonies. If Aliya Day is intended to offer some sort of encouragement, acknowledge our sacrifices, or at the bare minimum discourage olim from leaving, it probably falls short. It is hard to imagine that this law and the ceremonies that accompany it have an impact on olim's decision to stay or leave—regardless of their age.

Israel is hard on the best of days, even with a calendared Aliya Day that honors those who immigrated here. We are not the first to publicly admit that Israel is not for the faint-hearted, and we won't be the last. Even native Israelis leave, which means there are difficulties for everyone.

It's okay to complain about Israel and how hard it is to make aliya, but don't expect Israelis to feel sorry for you. There is also a difference between complaints that stem from frustration and complaints that sound like victimhood. The latter has no place in Israeli society, for the whole raison d'etre of Zionism is that we are no longer victims or subject to another country's largesse.

You chose it, you own it, but your aliya does come with a return receipt. And that brings us back to the tried and true "you can always go back" concept.

All olim have a honeymoon period, and it can last for a few years. For most olim, the "#OnlyInIsrael" moments are the high you live off of during the honeymoon period and sometimes beyond. But it might not be enough to pull you through the hard times.

⊘ Reality Check

The reality is that the aliya honeymoon will end. Olim need to learn the language, navigate their life in it, find a job, a place to live, a supportive community, friends, friends who become family, education systems for children, and stand up for themselves in ways they never did before. Along the way, olim often encounter some, or many, rough prickly Israelis in all elements of society, a rowdy bunch who will yell at you while claiming that "it isn't personal"—and it probably isn't. Native Israelis pride themselves on a trait that can grate on many olim, and that is brutal honesty. It is not always a pleasant experience being on the receiving end of that brutal honesty, which is often wrapped in an aggressive tone of voice. And, once again, it's not personal.

One of the best pieces of advice we received from friends who made aliya four years prior to us was this: "no" is only an opening suggestion; it isn't a final answer,[16] which reflects the kind of pushiness that is needed to survive in Israel. Never stop at no.

Real Israeli life starts when you love Israel for what it is, warts and all. Ultimately, that love does not put food on the table, help you earn a living wage, bring you closer to your family, absolve you from learning Hebrew, protect you from Israeli aggressiveness, or bring you comfort if you feel you were sold a bill of goods. Elements of Israeli life, like learning the language, becoming more assertive, seeking help when you need it, managing your expectations, and proactively looking for your right community or creating your own, are within olim's control.

Many of us can quote Herzl's famous line, "If you will it, it is no dream," but many can't recite the second half of that quote: "But, if you do not wish it, all this that I have related to you is and will remain a fable."[17] Herzl made it quite clear that you have to really want it and you have to have faith in it, because if you don't, it's a passion that fades, and it will remain only a myth, an unfulfilled legend.

The hard truth is that some olim never adjust, never culturally catch up, but those who really want to make it here accept that there will always be a deficiency. They accept their shortcomings, laugh at them occasionally, and get through the more complex moments by asking for help.

Someone once said that true love doesn't come by finding a perfect person but by learning to love an imperfect person perfectly. That sums up how olim should view Israel, and if you somehow can't accept that loving Israel is an imperfect thing, aliya is reversible without much of a penalty.

To the olim who decide to "go home," don't judge yourself too harshly. Take comfort in the fact that you are not alone, and your mere attempt to "live the aliya dream" is a feat unto itself. Every day that you lived in Israel was an accomplishment, a success. We are the "Start Up Nation," and we know better than most that failure is part of the innovation process, a stepping stone to success. Perhaps one day you will return. It has been known to happen.

To the parents of olim, if the aliya experiment did not succeed for your children, the "I told you so" refrain rubs salt into an open wound. Keep in mind that native Israelis also leave. Every day they managed to live in Israel was a success. The burden of failure doesn't rest solely on your children's shoulders, for there are a confluence of factors that make Israel a complex place to live. Give your children the credit for trying what was once only a dream.

Conclusions

"*With a Pained Body and Hungry Heart, This Is My Home*"

—*Ehud Manor[1]*

It is not lost on us that we doled out advice on communication, mutual respect, understanding, acceptance, and managing expectations—all concepts that are part and parcel of navigating familial relationships regardless of whether aliya is in the cards.

The difference is that aliya brings on a wave of different emotions and reactions that probably don't exist when people announce that they are moving *anywhere* else that is far away from their families. Family members' responses to Israel are different than, say, moving to a faraway place within one's home country or to another continent entirely.

It is the overwhelming set of emotions about aliya that causes such a wide range of reactions that otherwise would not be present for any other move. When olim announce their intentions to move to Israel, their family and friends might feel the same commitment to Israel but not enough to compel them to uproot their lives. The emotional approach to aliya is what can transform otherwise solid familial relationships into shaky ones, or shaky ones to bad ones.

Regardless of your age when you make aliya, the minute you announce your intentions, the relationships in your life start to fall into certain categories:

- **The Awestruck:** Those who are in awe of your decision and emotionally or financially support you wholeheartedly.

- **The Mildly Supportive:** Those who believe in Zionism, want the best for you, and generally agree that this is the right thing to do even if they won't follow you.

- **The Disparaging:** Those who constantly repeat stories of failure, how hard it is, and that you should have a backup plan.

■ **The Naysayers:** Those who don't believe you will ever make it there and actively discourage aliya.

Olim will be most helped by the awestruck and the mildly supportive, and these are relationships that will endure and stand the test of time many years after aliya. The disparaging or the naysayers will no longer be part of an oleh's life, if nothing else because it is just too hard to live in Israel, and these relationships are toxic to our ability to succeed.

The emotion aliya evokes for every oleh is not easy to recognize if you yourself don't have it. It is most similar to a chronic condition. If you don't suffer from a chronic condition, you can't possibly understand what it means to have it. We, and other olim, suffer from a chronic condition called Zionism. It is there all the time, it runs through our veins, and we move to Israel to cure it.

But most chronic conditions are only managed, not cured. Same for Zionism. You arrive as an oleh with great dreams. You breathe deeply for the first time. You walk the paths of our forefathers. You celebrate holidays with seven million other Jews who celebrate the very same holiday, albeit a bit differently. Slowly but surely, the aches and pains, like any chronic condition, creep back in. They are little nuisances, like bureaucracy, aggressiveness, and never-ending culture shock, and you make adjustments all the time to account for these aches and pains.

But then you have your #OnlyInIsrael moments, and it's a new panacea, like a booster shot—until the cycle starts all over again. And herein lies the truth. Aliya doesn't cure your Zionism; it manages it, and it is a lifelong process.

Those who make aliya really believe, in their bones, that they have no other country, no other place that is right for them. In fact, there is a melancholy song, "I Have No Other Country," written in the wake of Israel's War of Attrition. A rarely discussed historic event, this inconclusive war with Egypt[2] was meant to wear Israel down through a long engagement that would have dislodged Israeli forces from the Sinai Peninsula, seized during the 1967 Six Day War. It nearly became a battle between Israel and a great superpower at the time, the Soviet Union, but when Nassar died, Egyptian President Sadat didn't renew the fighting—at least at that time.

Many in the country felt the war had no purpose and that our soldiers died in vain. The song was written in memory of a lost soldier, but the lyrics reflect the complexity of Israel that most olim understand once the honeymoon period wears off:

> I have no other country
> Even if my land burns
> Only a word in Hebrew penetrates my veins and my soul
> With a pained body, with a hungry heart
> This is my home.
>
> I won't be silenced, because my land has changed its face
> I won't give up on her
> I will remind her
> I will sing here in her ears
> Until she opens her eyes

> אין לי ארץ אחרת
> גם אם אדמתי בוערת
> רק מילה בעברית חודרת אל ורקיי, אל נשמתי
> בגוף כואב, בלב רעב
> כאן הוא ביתי
>
> לא אשתוק, כי ארצי שינתה את פניה
> לא אוותר לה
> אזכיר לה
> ואשיר כאן באחוניה
> עד שתפקח את עיניה

This is what it means to want to stay in Israel—to feel that you have no other place to be; that it is our duty to build the modern state together; to acknowledge the cognitive dissonance that exists here; to understand the country's painful imperfections; to know that our land can burn with divisiveness; to accept that with sovereignty comes responsibility; and to believe that *kol yisrael arevim zeh la'zeh,* we are all connected to one another, even when we disagree or disagree vehemently. With a pained body and a hungry heart, as the song says, each and every one of us is committed to her, and we won't give up on her. Aliya isn't a starting point. It is a lifelong journey.

The emotional impact of moving to Israel is not lost on olim—in fact, it is what brings them to Israel to begin with. The truth is that aliya doesn't just affect olim. It touches the rest of the family left behind. For those left behind, aliya can result in a communication divide that grows wider and wider with time, but it does not have to be this way. We hope that this book bridges the emotional impact of aliya and narrows the gap between olim and their families.

Olim should not expect that their families will understand their Israeli life but, by the same token, families who did not make the journey with us should view our relationship with Israel as akin to a marriage.

We fell in love with Israel, so we married it. Staying in love with it meant that we've had a few fights, we worked out how to accept the good with the bad, and we are in the process of fixing some things around the edges to make it better for us and the generations to come.

Acknowledgments

We are deeply indebted to the two young adults in our lives who have made us feel inadequate every day, our children Bracha and Benjy Losice, who became Israeli citizens at the ages of 13 and 8, respectively. We are so incredibly proud of the Israelis you have become and even more proud that you somehow never looked back or uttered the words, "It was better in America." You did, of course, resort to the refrain we heard from so many other young olim, flinging about that phrase, "You just don't understand Israel." It forced us to try to dig deeper, to ask others for help, and to appreciate the fact that you will be more successful and a greater asset to the State of Israel than we could ever be.

Somewhere in the recesses of our minds, we knew the day would come when an ocean would separate us from our aging parents. In the years since we made aliya, Avi's parents, Rivka and Moshe Losice (זכרונם לברכה-of blessed memory), passed away. Ariella's parents continue to live in what she calls "the greatest Diaspora on earth," Lawrence, New York. For a few years before COVID-19 erupted, Ariella made the trip across the pond every three to four months just to check in. If you are fortunate to have parents alive and well in another country, the danger of air travel as of this writing only adds to the guilt of being unable to see parents as often as you want.

The Losice and Bernstein homes had an abundance of love and commitment to the State of Israel. Our parents remember well the day when the State of Israel was created. Yet, enthusiasm waned fast when we told our parents that we were making aliya. Both sets of parents expressed guarded support, well-hidden pride, and a poorly concealed critique of our decision to have Avi "commute" and work in the United States for more than five years.

They knew what was hard for us to fully accept, that there would be adverse consequences to Avi's American-based employment. No one could identify what those consequences would be or how our family would look down the road, but our parents were right. And we, adults of 40 and 48 respectively, were wrong, or at least we were not fully conscious of the impact of Avi's American employment. We truly believed we had enough life experience to push past the challenges and, since then, we have spent quite a bit of time recalibrating and creating a healthier family dynamic in Israel, but it turns out that our parents knew all along what we did not. And this, too, is a message for olim. Even as adults, your parents know you best. When they are concerned or give you unsolicited advice, it is only because they love you and want the best for you. We are forever grateful to our parents for their love, their guidance, and the values they instilled in us. We can only hope we have passed that torch onto the next generation.

As we mentioned numerous times throughout this book, olim make friends who become their family. Good friends have become our Israeli family. They are the ones we turned to for advice of all kinds, from health to education, the ones we lived with through the ups and downs of mini-wars as our children served. As with many friendships, our Israeli family developed through our children's educational frameworks.

On September 6, 2009, less than three weeks after we landed in Israel, we met Hannah Kanarek, mother of triplets and twins, the latter of which were in the same grade with our son Benjy. Ariella found her first job thanks to Hannah, and not only are we close friends but our children remain friends to this day.

We met Abby and Shalom Lipner through their daughter Elisheva, a classmate of our daughter Bracha. Ariella has yet to sufficiently internalize Elisheva's wise words—*"proportziot, Ariella"*—"keep things in perspective." It remains a work in progress.

Hannah, Abby, and Shalom are the people we turned to again and again for advice, guidance, and a reality check, and we are eternally grateful for their understanding, love, and friendship.

Our American home was always beset by nonstop action. Bracha's best friends Sheryl Green Wallin, Megan Barbanel, and Michal Hubert were "frequent flyers" at our home in the United States, as were Leah's friends, including Tammi Rabin, who made aliya with her husband Max and live in Jerusalem not far from us. We tried our best to recreate the same hustle and bustle atmosphere here in Israel because background noise makes our house a home. We live right across the street from Bracha's high school, which meant our kitchen was the lunch room with pancakes often prepared by classmates. And once Bracha graduated, it was Benjy's turn. Nearly every Shabbat from 9th through 12th grade, Benjy's friends Avichai, Avi, Yair, and Yona (the latter has been Benjy's best friend since kindergarten, our pilot year in Israel) have become part of our home's background noise. We would not have it any other way and are grateful for our children's friends who have made our Jerusalem house the home we wanted it to be.

A book of this nature required input very early, from two different groups—young olim and their parents. If this book is helpful at all, it is thanks to those who agreed to review the early manuscript and made very thoughtful recommendations. We are deeply indebted to Daniel Rosehill, LiAmi Lawrence, Avital Eusgeld, Jacob Rosenbaum, Corky Milworn, Michal Hubert, Shelley and Stephen Hubert, Daniel Adler, Rabbi Dr. Michael Reichel, and Rabbi Yehoshua Fass for taking precious time out of their lives to make this book the best it can be.

Our eternal gratitude goes to Fern Reiss, our publishing consultant. When we reached out to Fern, we told her there was no market for this book, yet we were determined to write it nonetheless. Fern believed in us; she believed in this endeavor every step of the way; and she believed in this book's usefulness for others, even when we weren't quite so sure. We are grateful for every suggestion Fern made and, more importantly, for pushing us to meet our own deadlines.

Arielle Kwestel, our book designer, brought the manuscript to life, and we are honored to have worked with such a talented—and patient—designer who understood our vision from the get-go.

We would be remiss if we did not thank the many young olim who have grown to be part of our extended family. This book was born largely because of our experiences with you. Your passion for your place in Israel reignites the very same feelings we had the day we landed in August 2009. We look forward to seeing all of you settled into your "adult" life and watching you struggle with very ordinary parental challenges as you raise your children in a complicated but beloved country. Your children will be "sabras," Israeli-born, and while we don't wish it on anyone, you might very well reap what you have sown and hear those famous last words, "Ima/Abba, you just don't understand Israel."

Finally, to the parents of idealistic olim, we all can agree that raising children is hard. Raising young adults who begin to chafe at parenting altogether is even harder. Raising young adults with seemingly naïve and endless passion for a country perpetually in conflict is yet harder still. Heavy majorities of olim and parents we surveyed indicated that their families were very committed to Zionism. Nearly 78% of olim and 84% of parents said that their families strongly identified with Zionism, supporting the notion that olim are raised in families that, perhaps unwittingly, fostered aliya. Your children did not grow up in a vacuum. They grew up in your home with your values, which they brought to this country to become citizens of the modern State of Israel, a privilege most of our grandparents did not have. They are this country's future, and together with their "sabra" friends and their "sabra" children, they will make you proud.

Even if Israelis never say it to you, we certainly will. Israel is a better place because your children are here.

Ariella Bernstein and Avi Losice
Jerusalem, Israel
March, 2021

Appendices

Appendix A: Survey Analysis

A total of 294 people responded to the survey we distributed; of them, 224 are (or were) young olim and 70 are parents of olim. The survey was publicized between June and September 2020 numerous times in a wide variety of Facebook groups and was sent to family and friends to distribute more broadly.

None of the questions were mandatory; therefore, respondents could skip any question they chose not to answer. The results noted here and throughout the book are weighted. Some questions were added during the surveying process based on suggestions from early responders. We filtered a number of questions by respondent type (oleh or parent) to better understand the differences between their views. When survey questions were posed with Likert scale responses, we tended to band together strongly agree/agree and strongly disagree/disagree.

The sample size is small; it is not self-selecting or a representative sample of olim to Israel. Therefore, survey analysis is for general informational purposes only. There are occasions where rounding caused results to fall slightly above or slightly below 100%. We used the data results as a basis for our conclusions in this book, and all analysis was done in good faith based on the answers provided.

1. Country of Origin:

75% of respondents were from the United States. The remainder were from Canada, Europe, South Africa, Australia, and Central and South America. These numbers are not representative of the official aliya statistics because we captured only English-language olim and their families.

2. Age on first trip to Israel

	Olim	Parents
Before the age of 5	38%	7%
Ages 6-10	20%	10%
Ages 11-18	34%	49%
Ages 19-25	6%	23%
Ages 26-30	1%	3%
Over 31	0	8%

The data tends to show that 58% olim visited Israel for the first time at younger ages (before the age of 10). Overwhelmingly, the data supports the notion that olim respondents made their first trip to Israel before the age of 18.

3. Frequency of visits to Israel

	Olim	Parents
Once a year	22%	31%
2-4 times/year	5%	26%
5 or more times a year	4%	2%
Every 2-3 years	50%	38%
Visited 1x in my life	19%	3%

4. Did the oleh have a college degree prior to making aliya?

Yes: 25%
No: 75%

5.   Did you discuss completing a college degree before aliya?

	Olim	Parents
Yes	50%	59%
No	50%	41%

6.   A question was dedicated to why a college degree arose as part of aliya discussions. The question allowed selection of multiple answers. A total of 258 responses were received. The following breaks down the responses:

Follow cultural or family norms to complete an education	91
Did not come up	75
Increasing professional success	61
Backup plan	40
Aliya was made post-degree so the issue didn't come up	37
Planned on getting a degree at "home" but stayed in Israel after gap year	36
Aliya was planned intentionally after university degree	33
Support the notion that Israelis appreciate degrees from prestigious institutions	19
Aliya was made to start studies in Israel	18

Even though 75 respondents indicated that the issue did not come up at all, 183 respondents selected more than one answer, indicating that the subject arose in one way or another. The multiplicity of answers from most respondents suggests that during these discussions, the issue came up from multiple angles. Among some of the free text comments, a few (4) mentioned that there were discussions about the lack of English language university programs.

7.   To what extent do you agree with this statement? There was a concern that attending university was not part of a post-aliya plan.

Strongly agree	10%
Agree	21%
Don't recall	13%
Disagree	35%
Strongly disagree	22%

8.   What were the reasons for making aliya? The question allowed respondents to select multiple answers. A total of 263 responses were received, averaging more than 3½ answers per respondent. The following is the breakdown of responses:

Very strong feelings/destiny of wanting to live in Israel	200
Jews belong in Israel	167
Inspiration to live in a place where everyone shares the same culture	140
Defend the country	134
An inspiring gap year	108
It's awesome	87
Others did it before and success can be replicated	34

A majority of respondents led with "destiny-related answers" (strong feelings of wanting to live in Israel, Jews belong in Israel, or they were inspired to live in a Jewish cultural place). Only 10 respondents indicated that they came to defend the country alone. No one said "it was awesome" alone. Among some of the free text comments submitted, a handful (8) indicated that they moved to Israel to escape antisemitism, and 3 added that they came to Israel to marry a Jew.

9.   To what extent do you agree with this statement? There are challenges associated with making aliya.

Nearly 100% of olim and parents indicated that they agreed or strongly agreed with the statement that there are challenges associated with aliya.

10.   To what extent do you agree with this statement? Challenges associated with aliya were discussed between parents and olim.

	Olim	Parents
Strongly Agree	19%	35%
Agree	45%	47%
Don't know	15%	3%
Disagree	15%	12%
Strongly disagree	6%	3%

When banding the two "agreement" categories, 82% of parents agreed vs. 64% of olim. The larger difference was in the strongly agree category, where parents are far more certain than olim that they discussed the challenges (16% difference).

11.   To what extent do you agree with this statement? Aliya discussions between parents and oleh were limited because they became frustrating.

Strongly Agree	6%
Agree	15%
Don't know	11%
Disagree	40%
Strongly disagree	30%

There was little difference between olim and parents in their answers. About 20% report that the discussions about aliya were frustrating, but an overwhelming percentage, 70%, don't agree or strongly disagree that discussions about aliya were limited because they were frustrating.

12. To what extent do you agree with this statement? Aliya discussions between parents and olim were limited because neither side understood the other.

	Olim	Parents
Strongly Agree	5%	3%
Agree	12%	2%
Don't know	17%	5%
Disagree	27%	34%
Strongly disagree	39%	57%

91% of parents disagree with the above sentiment. While most olim also disagreed (66%), the gap between parents and olim (25%) demonstrates an "understanding gap." That sentiment is supported by the fact that 17% of olim agree that there were limited discussions because neither side understood the other, 12% higher than parents.

13. If concerns about aliya were raised, what were they? A total of 266 people responded to this multiple-choice question:

No concerns expressed	77
Too far away from family	129
We won't see each other too often	99
Can't make a living	66
Get an education first	64
It's expensive	55
Army service	43
You won't make it without assistance	38
It's dangerous	30
Start your career first	22
People we know left Israel	12
Didn't discuss with parents	12

Setting aside those who said that no concerns were expressed, respondents ticked off an average of 3 concerns.

14.   To what extent do you agree with this statement? Once a decision was made about aliya, "next steps" were openly discussed (next steps = anything—i.e., the application process, IDF, National Service, university, places to live, etc.).

	Olim	Parents
Strongly Agree	40%	69%
Agree	29%	21%
Don't know or don't remember	14%	1%
Disagree	11%	9%
Strongly disagree	6%	0%

The data shows that parents have a much stronger view of how much decision making was shared with them after a decision was made regarding aliya. About 40% of olim strongly agree that they discussed "next steps" in Israel with their parents, compared to nearly 70% of parents.

15. On Aliya Day, did olim and parents travel and remain together at the airport prior to boarding?

Yes	67%
No	10%
Made aliya in Israel	13%
No for logistical reasons	10%

16. To what extent do you agree with this statement? Following aliya, olim consulted with parents prior to signing official documents (i.e., bank forms, credit card forms, army forms, education-related forms, or rental agreements).

	Olim	Parents
Strongly Agree	13%	16%
Agree	10%	20%
Some yes, some no	42%	46%
Disagree	23%	15%
Strongly disagree	12%	3%

Olim and parents mostly agree with one another that consultation occurred on some issues but not others. However, the data also tends to show that parents think they are being consulted more often (36% of parents agree/strongly agree) when olim represent that they are not (45% strongly disagree/disagree).

17. Following aliya, when monetary issues arose, how often were there discussions between oleh and parents?

	Olim	Parents
Often	27%	34%
Occasionally	42%	53%
Rarely	21%	9%
Never	10%	4%

87% of parents believe that their children discuss monetary issues with them (often or occasionally), compared to 69% of olim. Olim consult their parents with some regularity but not quite as much as the parents believe. About 31% of olim report that they rarely or never discuss monetary issues with their parents, compared to 13% of parents. The data tends to show that parents think that they are consulted on monetary issues more often than they actually are.

18. To what extent do you agree with this statement? Prior to IDF or National Service, sufficient information was available about service options. (Data for this question was filtered only for those who served.)

	Olim	Parents
Strongly agree	16%	4%
Agree	37%	50%
Disagree	36%	35%
Strongly disagree	11%	10%

Nearly half of parents (45%) and olim (47%) disagree that they had sufficient information prior to service (banded disagree and strongly disagree). It is troubling to see such a high percentage of olim and parents believe that they lacked sufficient information when they probably thought that they were well informed enough.

19. To what extent do you agree with this statement? During IDF or National Service, the oleh received appropriate care. (Data for this question was filtered only for those who served.)

	Olim	Parents
Strongly agree	16%	12%
Agree	53%	68%
Disagree	23%	15%
Strongly disagree	9%	5%

Among olim, nearly one third (32%) indicated that they did not receive appropriate care (banded disagree and strongly disagree). It suggests that this data might be a subset of those above who feel they did not have sufficient information about their service. If they believe they did not recieve appropriate care during service, it can explain why they believe they did not have sufficient information *prior* to service.

20. To what extent do you agree with this statement? My feelings about IDF or National Service changed after service completion. (Data for this question was filtered only for those who served.)

	Olim	Parents
Strongly agree	25%	11%
Agree	38%	41%
Disagree	23%	39%
Strongly disagree	15%	11%

About 63% of olim indicated that their feelings about their service changed when they completed it, compared to 52% of parents. The 9% differential can be explained by the fact that olim might have had higher expectations of their service at the outset. We did not ask whether the changes in sentiment were positive or negative in nature.

21. To what extent do you agree with this statement? Parents know where their children spend holidays/ weekends.

	Olim	Parents
Strongly Agree	23%	38%
Agree	37%	38%
Don't know/not sure	25%	18%
Strongly disagree	15%	6%

Most olim (60%) agree that their parents know where they spend their weekends or holidays. More parents (76%) think that they know where their children are on weekends or holidays. About a quarter of parents (24%) aren't sure or don't know where their children are or strongly disagree with the sentiment that they know where their children spend their weekends or holidays.

22. To what extent do you agree with this statement? Parents can name at least two families that olim visited regularly.

	Olim	Parents
Strongly Agree	23%	40%
Agree	36%	42%
Don't know/not sure	28%	15%
Strongly disagree	13%	3%

More than 80% of the parents report that they can name at least two families olim visit regularly, compared to 59% of olim, nearly the same percentage of olim who think their parents know where they spend their weekends (question #21). The data from the former question coupled with this one demonstrates, in our view, that parents who know where their children spend their time also seem to be active listeners and retain the names of their children's hosts.

23. To what extent do you agree with this statement? Post-aliya, communication between parents and olim took place at least once a week ("communication" = WhatsApp, FB messenger, Telegram, phone calls, or e-mail).

	Olim	Parents
Strongly Agree	71%	83%
Agree	18%	15%
Don't know	3%	0%
Disagree	5%	2%
Strongly disagree	3%	0%

Nearly all parents (98%) strongly agree/agree that post-aliya communication takes place at least weekly. Nearly 90% of olim (89%) share the sentiment, but around 10% disagree or don't know. The wide variety of communication media probably helps to increase frequency of contact.

24. To what extent do you agree with this statement? After aliya, parents ultimately accepted their children's independence.

	Olim	Parents
Strongly Agree	50%	65%
Agree	36%	32%
Not sure	9%	2%
Disagree	3%	2%
Strongly disagree	2%	0%

Overwhelmingly, both olim and their parents strongly agree/agree that after aliya, parents accept olim's independence. Very few olim or parents disagree, but some aren't sure.

25. To what extent do you agree with this statement? Pre- and post-aliya discussions were productive.

	Olim	Parents
Strongly Agree	29%	49%
Agree	41%	43%
Don't know/can't recall	15%	4%
Disagree	11%	4%
Strongly disagree	4%	0%

More than 90% of parents (92%) found the discussions productive, compared to 70% of olim, a more than 20% gap. There is a far higher percentage of olim who disagree or don't know/don't recall if their pre- and post-aliya discussions were productive (30%), compared to parents (8%), suggesting that parents *believe* these aliya conversations to be more productive than olim claim they are.

26. To what extent do you agree with this statement? Pre-aliya discussions were tense, but after the decision was made they improved.

	Olim	Parents
Strongly Agree	6%	6%
Agree	22%	26%
Don't know/can't recall	20%	11%
Disagreed	27%	37%
Strongly disagree	25%	20%

Both population groups agree or disagree to a similar degree; about 30% of both population groups strongly agree/agree that discussions were tense and improved following the decision; and about 50% strongly disagree/disagree. Because this question was compounded, it is difficult to conclude which portion of the question they agreed or disagree with and, therefore, interpretation of the response is more difficult.

27. To what extent do you agree with this statement? Pre-aliya discussions were open, but they were tense post-aliya.

	Olim	Parents
Strongly Agree	0%	0%
Agree	6%	11%
Don't know/can't recall	14%	12%
Disagree	42%	39%
Strongly disagree	37%	37%

As with the prior question, answers here are open to interpretation. They could have focused on the openness or the tension. Olim agree with the statement much more than parents do, and parents disagree much more than olim do. One could assume that more olim believed that post-aliya discussions were tense, and more parents disagreed with that notion.

28. To what extent do you agree with this statement? There were barely any pre-aliya discussions.

	Olim	Parents
Strongly Agree	10%	1%
Agree	18%	11%
Don't know/can't recall	17%	10%
Disagree	27%	39%
Strongly disagree	28%	39%

Majorities of parents (78%) and olim (55%) both strongly disagree/disagree that there were barely any pre-aliya discussions. The gap between them suggests that some of these discussions might have been more meaningful to the parents but were less so, or unremarkable, for olim.

29.   To what extent do you agree with this statement? All along, discussions about aliya were frustrating.

	Olim	Parents
Strongly Agree	4%	2%
Agree	6%	5%
Don't know/can't recall	14%	9%
Disagree	24%	35%
Strongly disagree	52%	49%

Among both olim and parents, a small group, no more than 10%, found aliya discussions frustrating. Both olim (76%) and parents (84%) largely disagreed.

30.   Of olim respondents who served in some capacity, the following is their service breakdown:

National Service: 29%
IDF: 71%

31.   Do you know of anyone who made aliya who left Israel within 5 years and if so, under what circumstances? This question was open-ended, leaving respondents free to enter what they wished.   A total of 113 responses were received.

	Olim	Parents	Total
Yes	94	19	113
Of which the following left for these reasons			
Economic/financial	42	7	49
After IDF service	20	1	21
Nonintegration/culture	34	5	39
Distance from family	27	2	29
Security/danger	4	1	5

32.   Which sentence best describes you at the time of aliya?

	Olim	Parents
Parents and oleh had same level of religiosity	60%	72%
Oleh was more religiously committed than parents	26%	23%
Oleh was less religiously committed than parents	14%	5%

33.   Did your level of religiosity change after aliya? There were 131 respondents who answered this open question.

	Olim	Parents	Total
Yes, there were changes	57	12	69
Of which:			
Gave no indication whether it was more or less religious	23	7	30
More religious	13	3	16
Less religious	21	2	23
No	38	24	62

More than half of respondents did not answer this question, but half of those who did indicated that there was *some* change in religiosity after aliya, even more so from the stance of olim. It seems clear from parental responses that their answers reflected their thoughts on their own children. It is hard to extrapolate the meaning behind a "yes" response, for it can mean someone who became more religious or less so.

34. Family identification with Zionism

	Olim	Parents
Very committed	77%	84%
Slightly committed	17%	13%
Apathetic	2%	2%
Not committed	3%	1%
Against	0%	0%

No more than 5% of either group characterized their family as apathetic or not committed to Zionism. Heavy majorities of both groups say that families were very committed to Zionism. It supports the notion that olim are raised in families that demonstrated their commitment to Zionism and fostered aliya, perhaps unwittingly.

35. Knowing what you know today, what advice would you give yourself, parents, or others about aliya?

Oleh responses:

- Think twice about joining the IDF at 24. Try to find a better job.
- Be prepared for anything and everything.
- It's important to know and be confident in your reasons because it definitely isn't easy, but ultimately אם תרצו אין זו אגדה
- If you're sure you want to do it, don't wait, come as young as you can.
- Do it when you are really ready, make sure to take the steps to prepare first.
- Find yourself an adopted family before coming to Israel,

someone who will invite you over for Shabbat, who can give advice on rentals, who connects you to Israelis. Try to connect with actual people (not advisors) before coming.

- Try to get prepared ahead of time as much possible. Find a support network and don't be afraid to ask for help.
- Take time learning the language thoroughly before you come to Israel.
- Make more of an effort to keep in touch with family.
- Do proper research to understand if this is the right decision for you.
- Everything in life is scary and yes, it's a big move, but it's 100% worth it.
- Talk about the important things they don't teach you anywhere, like how to open a bank account and how do you deal with bank problems, what you should look for when you're visiting apartments to rent, how to look for a job.
- A trip makes things look fun, but once you become a citizen, that's when s*** hits the fan. You are in a downward spiral of depression because of how hard Israel makes it for her citizens.
- You are going through a big transition now so come with an open mind.
- Try to build connections with families/friends prior to aliya and have an open discussion with them about how they may be able to lend you a hand while you're an oleh chadash. Understand before drafting that the army will be a huge sacrifice. Serving should be a value of yours, but you can't depend on the army to take care of you.
- Learn Hebrew, have a Plan B, learn the culture! Don't stay in your bubble or comfort zone. Make mistakes because that is the way you learn. Smile, you are at home ☺.
- I am two years post-aliya. My parents financially cut me off

and I remain financially independent. You cannot live your life for your parents. You need to do what's best for you. They act the way they do because they love and miss you in ways you won't understand until you're a parent. Don't give up your dreams because of it, but understand where they are coming from.

- If you have a gut feeling for Israel, go for it. However, be smart about it. Learn as much Hebrew as possible. Constantly try and improve in your verbal, written, and writing skills.
- Don't move to the periphery. Come with a remote job.
- Don't stress!!!! What will be will be, and never stop pushing for what you want!!! Don't be afraid to speak!!!
- Aliya is hard, it's hard for everyone, both parents and the young adults who go through it. That being said, it is the best decision I have ever made and although my parents hated the idea at first, they've grown to not only accept it but be proud of my decision and accomplishments.
- Let a child decides what's best for them.
- Talk to everybody for the sake of your Hebrew and for the sake of expanding your knowledge.
- Have a support system, don't be afraid to ask for help. Be open to feedback and meeting new people.
- Finish your paperwork and have a solid plan.
- Commit to the language, join the army and be realistic. It's going to be really really hard and frustrating. Don't expect it to be fantastic, it will only stress you out when it isn't.
- Earlier is better and an easier transition. Getting your degree here is easier for integration later on.
- Have a better plan.
- Don't make a plan. Make an outline. Especially if you're coming pre-university. People plan and plan, but at the end of the day, things rarely go the way you think they will. Not

being prepared for bumps makes things a lot harder. I see olim struggle with this all the time.

- It's really hard work. But it's so rewarding. Advocate for yourself. Don't be afraid to ask for help.
- Don't expect it to be just like home, because it will never feel 100% like home.
- Start as early as possible; it takes a long time.
- Do your research before coming—about jobs, the health care system, daily life in Israel, communities in Israel.
- It's a process, and it's hard to say goodbye, but in this world of technology, it is so much easier to stay in touch with those left behind.
- Distance is not as much of an issue because of WhatsApp/video calls. While there are terror attacks, they don't physically affect the whole country. It's safer than one thinks.
- Even if your parents disagree with your choice, they still love you and would rather have a relationship with you from afar than none at all.
- Think it through, learn the language, make sure you have support (preferably both in Israel and abroad). If you can, spend a year rather than a week on a pilot trip (year abroad, that kind of thing). Try to get to know daily life, not just filtered through a program. And brush up on your grocery/shopping vocabulary—it'll help a *lot.* Try to connect with other olim, especially experienced ones. Find an Israeli friend who is happy to help you with phrasing/understanding can be invaluable. Put a dictionary app on your phone, and don't be afraid to use it in university/stores/wherever.
- The adjustment process will take time, so be patient with yourself. Living in Israel will add to your religious connection overall but not every day. Feeling connected to

Torah still will take a lot of effort, and you will need to make the effort to find like-minded people.

■ It is overwhelming at first, but it gets better.

■ Make sure you always have a community you feel comfortable in, but not too comfortable such that you aren't learning.

■ It's a long process to become fully part of the country and understand how everything works—and that's ok!

■ There are a lot of challenges. It's not a decision to be made lightly.

■ Enjoy the process, it goes by very quickly. Be open with your parents about your experiences.

■ Do your research!!! You can never be 100% sure about aliya. When it occurs to you 80% of the time, it's time to move. Be open to change. Aliya will be challenging, but nothing great comes from staying in one's comfort zone.

■ Don't be afraid to ask questions to anyone who is willing to listen. The more information you have, the better.

■ Take all the opportunities you can to integrate.

■ Do your research before discussing the army as an option. It was 3 years of my life I deeply regret but at the same time a mistake I was glad to have made. If you are going to make aliya (alone not with family), ask the kid to do a gap year or Masa program first, get the feeling of living in the country before you make a permanent decision because a two-week trip Taglit trip is different than a 9-month program immersing yourself in society first.

■ Support and open conversation.

■ Don't assume that the information you receive is correct. Just because someone sounds convincing or because they are in a position of authority does not mean that they are providing you with the correct information.

■ Make sure you have a solid support system in Israel...at

least one place where you feel absolutely comfortable going at any time, helpful if you have a key, a place where you know you can feel good and be taken care of.

■ Support your kids.

■ Really think if it's the right decision for you. Don't do it because others (religious teachers, etc.) encourage it. The reality of living in Israel isn't a piece of cake. Socially it can be very difficult. It is important to integrate into Israeli society. Don't live in an Anglo bubble.

■ If you believe in Zionism, participate in it actively and not passively or from far away.

■ Figure out as much as you can, but also know that nothing is really known. Hard work pays off.

■ Remember you are not the only one to go through what you are going through now. Don't be afraid to say that it is getting hard for you.

■ I really do believe it's the only option for Jews. And while obviously we can't all live in Israel, it should be something we are all constantly planning for. There are so many ways to make it here and you are all capable.

■ It's not easy, but if you have good support from friends and family it's doable even on your own. Your new friends become your family.

■ Ask people you know, who live in Israel and ENJOY living in Israel, for advice and info.

■ Recognize that making aliya means becoming an immigrant (it might sound silly to say), regardless of the amount of "cushions" we receive, even if you are familiar with the land/people/culture/language. It is still hard, but everyone adjusts in their own way and at their own pace.

■ It is a stressful process but once it is through, you'll start to feel like you're at home again. There are always struggles, but what got me through it all was taking a deep breath and just doing it.

- It's the hardest but best decision you'll ever make.

- Overall, I think my expectations going into it were realistic and there isn't anything I would tell myself differently. Perhaps what to pack, or random bureaucratic things, but those things are sometimes dependent on location so it wouldn't qualify as regular advice.

- Living in Israel is not the same as caring for and visiting Israel. Culturally I have more in common with the average non-Jew in Toronto than the average Israeli Jew.

- If you want to do it and you can show your parents that you're committed and believe in what you're doing, then they'll support you eventually.

- Make sure you're mentally prepared to face a non-native language, an expensive country, and that things won't always go your way. There are people willing to help and there also are people who aren't willing.

- Having your own "people" who can look after you and help you. People you can rely on makes a huge difference. The best thing for you to do is to secure as many personal accounts as possible from those who have done it before.

- Do it, but be realistic about the obstacles. It may be hard in the beginning, but it'll be super worthwhile.

- It can be done easily if proper measures are taken and you are flexible.

- Trust your child even if it is not the path you would choose for him/her.

- It's not easy to live here. Especially if you're used to a level of comfort and convenience like the US. If you, like I, are less interested in comfort, then Israel is a wonderfully challenging place to grow and live. Anyone who wants to feel Israeli while living in Israel should do the army.

- Recognize that it is a privilege to live in Israel and take that into consideration when deciding to make aliya. Think what you will do with your privilege while here. There are Arabs who grew up and live in Jerusalem who want citizenship, and the process for them is MUCH harder than it is for an international Jew.

- Although I loved my university studies in England, I think studying in Israel and doing *Sherut Leumi*/army would have helped with building social networks and proficiency in Hebrew.
- It is hard but worth it!
- Don't be afraid to ask for help. Aliya is difficult; there is no shame in reaching out and using the network or benefits that you have.
- Having your parents' support (not financial but emotional) makes a huge difference in being able to thrive here.
- Plan. Talk to as many people who were in your shoes as you can before and after aliya.
- Contact family you have in Israel to be there for you even if it's distant.
- Don't worry too much about planning in advance. Things seem to come up and you need to learn to cope with changes.
- Getting a degree before aliya, in my case, was a good decision. Aliya is so much easier than it was in my day. Kids today have such an easier time communicating with family back home and getting their benefits than we did. Create your own family here. Aliya was the best thing I ever did.
- To young olim: Speak to your parents. I almost made aliya against my parents' will, but I decided to take the long route and speak to them and convince them. It wasn't easy. I was 19, it was 34 years ago when the conditions in Israel were far from perfect, but I was convinced that it was the right thing to do. Thank god I had the sense to keep the

channels of communication open with my parents. It took them 15 years, but they made aliya as well.

- Discuss things thoroughly, but don't expect it all to come about as you expect.

- Children (0-12): Younger is usually easier. From 12 through 18 it is very difficult. From 18 and on even harder.

- I've been here for 20 years, NBN did not exist, so I found out everything on my own. It's much different now. It's also easier to come when single without children. I see friend's children struggling with the change of culture and language.

- I think making aliya at the right time can make all the difference, and there is not much benefit to doing a degree in America beforehand. If anything, it makes things more complicated when wanting to continue into higher education.

- To olim: You have to be passionate about coming, because the challenges you experience in Israel aren't the same as anywhere else. Ask for help when you need it. Do *ulpan* before starting Israeli school. Save your aliya money. At the end of the day, no matter how much research you do, there will be more to find out once you land.

- Making aliya is like marriage: You have to go into it intending it to be for life.

- Approach aliya with open eyes, realistic expectations, and much flexibility.

- The younger the better. I made aliya after seminary when I was an unattached single with few responsibilities and started my adult life here. I see today how much easier that was than for those coming later in life.

- Perseverance is key. It's tough but worth every step :).

- Ask Israelis for help and connect to other olim vatikim (those who have been in Israel longer) from the beginning.

- Not relevant. My family pushed me to make aliya, so I had

a very different situation.

- It is not as scary as you think it is.
- If it is meant to be, things will work out.
- Personal decision, don't do it to please (or irritate) anyone else.
- Focus more on Hebrew even at the expense of a good first job.
- Try going as young as possible.
- Talk about it, talk about your fears, challenges, and about strategies to overcome them.
- Go only if you have to. It could have gone so wrong for me in Israel multiple times.
- If possible, learn as much Hebrew as you can before making aliya. Definitely don't listen to anyone who says it's not important because "everyone speaks English." It's essential to be independent and being part of a community. Be emotionally prepared to have to stand up for yourself every day. "No" really means "convince me," which is both good and bad. Truly throw away the notions of how things should be and work with what they are.
- Make a list of pros and cons and make sure you're making aliya for the right reasons.
- Keep the lines of communication open. Visit often.
- I should have stuck with my gut and made aliya when I originally wanted to. I should also have made aliya to the IDF and researched more about the army.
- Don't do it.
- Use all the resources you have, meet new people, and always pay attention to trends—where are the good places to hang out, which degrees are more useful, etc.
- Wow, a lot of things.
  1. Israel is a wonderful country but it's hard, too, so you need to know that you must work hard (Hebrew,

work, studies...).

2. Don't be afraid. You just need to jump in.
3. Have fun and enjoy, don't let anyone make your decisions for you because you are here, and no one else knows how it feels.
4. Have good communication with your family because there are going to be times that you will miss them, times when you will want go back. You will feel alone. You will cry and it's fine, you just need to know that you can do everything!
5. Have Israeli friends, go out with them, learn about them and know their culture, don't be shy if you made a mistake in Hebrew.
6. Welcome to Israel!

- Parents should try to understand the drive to make aliya.
- It's going to be hard on you in ways you don't yet realize. Challenges you know of will be harder than you expect.
- Keep as many options open as you can, whether it's SATs before you draft or doing as many *miyunim* for the army as you can, or applying to as many universities as you can.
- Come thinking it is permanent and you will succeed.
- If you don't have any family or support in Israel, don't come. If you can't support yourself to a reasonable standard of living, don't come.
- It's difficult, but if you're coming for the right reasons, you will succeed.
- Don't make stupid decisions at the age of 18, and complete your education before making aliya unless there are special circumstances.
- Don't do it without a good amount of savings.
- Come with good Hebrew or a realistic amount of time to learn Hebrew. If you are going to live in Israel without your parents, you should really be able to handle all parts of the

aliya and living in Israel process without your parents help, and if you can't then you are not ready to make aliya.

- One critical piece of advice is never compare Israel to your country of origin. Israel is a wonderful, scary, fantastic place to live and you are likely living here under different circumstances. We tend to shine a rosy light on our past memories and Israel, for the most part, can't live up to them. If you come as an 18- to 19-year-old, your memories are of a child—you had limited responsibilities—and they will only taint your experience. If you come as a 21- to 24-year-old, your memories are of a student—you were living in academia—and there is always a shock returning to real life after experiences like that.

- There are so many things that you only figure out after moving here. There is never enough information, everyone makes mistakes, and the whole experience can be amazingly frustrating. But you learn a lot as you go, and it's worth it in the end. You just need to keep moving forward.

- Being a lone soldier can be the best sometimes. It also depends what unit you are in. My unit is one of the best for lone soldiers, girls and boys, but it can be a little frustrating when no one really understands how you're feeling (if you miss your parents, if you're stressed out about medical stuff or even moving). Communication can also be affected if you are a combat soldier because your schedule can mean that you in locations where telephones don't work. Other than that, I really enjoy living in Israel and love my position in the army.

- Since aliya was about me, I decided to keep it to myself once I knew that I was seriously considering it. My parents knew how happy I was in Israel but were surprised when "the conversation" happened because I hadn't really talked about it with them. When I finally told them, I worked with a mental health professional for a few months to make sure I was thinking about this for the right reasons and not just getting wrapped up in the seminary year hype. Only one of my close friends knew how serious it was. That time gave me the chance to really listen to people's experiences and develop a solid plan. By the time I approached my parents I had a plan for the next 3-5 years. Spend some time with family prior to aliyah, *ulpan*, Sherut Leumi and I had an idea of positions I wanted to explore, *mechina* and university. I also knew where I wanted to live and why. I'm not saying don't talk to anyone about your thoughts for your future, just make sure they are the right people. They should challenge and support you during the process. My mom also noted that: "When I talked to people about the aliya of their kids, I realized you didn't really ask. You informed." And she's right. If you have to ask, you're still not sure. I knew this was what was best for me and hoped my parents would support me.

- I think it's important to recognize that as of the mid-20s, an adult child might really be an independent adult, possibly married, and the parents might be completely supportive of the adult child making aliya.
- Facebook groups were a great source of information for me.
- Honestly, I was moving back as an adult rather than coming for the first time/for the first time after spending minimal time in the country previously. I've thus avoided some challenges that other new olim face, or had them tempered, but still faced others. One thing everyone should know is that it'll take you a few years (or longer) to really get settled. It takes time to adjust, even with a lot of knowledge and help, and it can be tough, including emotionally. Be smart, make an informed decision about moving, how you are going to do it, and take care of yourself.

- As someone who made aliya as a single adult, I didn't know how the dating scene and singles communities differed than what I knew in NY. If there were resources on these differences in advance, I think that would have been helpful.

- I was the first to come to Israel. Then all of them came to Israel and today 24 members of my family are part of Israeli society.

- Something that helps is care packages from home. There are food products and medicine that I cannot get here and it makes me so happy to get these comforts.

- I would want to give advice to other potential olim who at times sound like they are expecting some kind of fairytale life here. I'd want to tell them that this country is tough and not like the vacation trips you took here. You will always be (most cases) a step behind as an immigrant. My best piece of advice is to have a sense of humor and always assume anything, at any office, will not be efficient or take several trips/days. This way, when it takes less time, you have exceeded expectations. I think you need to know yourself, what kind of life you want to lead, and why you want to come. This sort of honesty can help you prepare and hopefully determine if your goals and dreams are realistic. Last but not least, Israelis are tough but all heart. Don't be put off by people being pushy. The love, care, and family you have once you are here are worth the frustrating moments.

- My parents always supported Israel. We spent a lot of holidays in Israel and have a lot of family in Israel, so it was always engrained in me to move here. But once it became a reality, my parents were afraid of the distance, though they supported the decision.

- When I came, there was no e-mail or Facebook or

WhatsApp. Phone calls were so expensive we could only talk for a few minutes a week. Much easier now!

- In my opinion, aliya is much easier today. There are organizations such as NBN that help with almost every aspect, and communication with family abroad is quick, easy, and cheap. One of the main things olim can do to prepare is to learn Hebrew. I see teenagers who make aliya who aren't fluent in Hebrew, and that makes the process much more frustrating for them.

- We lived in Israel when I was a very young child and ever since, I maintained that I would "come home." My parents were very supportive and when the time was right, I came.

- Working with banks and *kupat cholim* (health care system) is a huge challenge.

- If you plan to live in Israel long term, it makes sense to get your degree/training in Israel and integrating from the beginning of your career instead of dealing with cultural differences and technical red tape later.

- From what I have experienced since my aliya, there are two main groups within young olim. Those who come from privileged first world countries, and those who don't. I see a lot of similarities in the types of struggles between olim from the US/France/Canada that I don't relate to, especially concerning work and salaries expectations. People who speak native English have a lot of job opportunities that are not open to the rest of us, regardless of our proficiency in the language.

- Aliyah and service as a lone soldier in the 1980s are MUCH different than today. We barely communicated with our parents. We got 3 aerograms and one 10-minute phone call on a shared army line a month. There was no Internet. There was no access to the outside world, and if we were not on base, the only way to reach parents was via pay phone.

- One thing I'm still trying to figure out is how Israeli or American I feel, where is the balance and the effects of trying to find that balance. This is an important variable to study. Dating trends should be observed. I know several cases of young adults who made aliya, immediately started dating, got engaged very fast, and got divorced several years later. This trend is important to pay attention to and address.

- Communication in those days was via snail mail, nothing like today.

- My parents were very supportive along the way. I did have my sister in Israel so it made it easier when I arrived. My parents recently made aliya, 8.5 years after my arrival and 9.5 years after my sister.

- Question number 15 (on frequency of communication with parents) is frustrating. I made aliya way before any of those things (e-mail, WhatsApp, etc.) were available. We used snail mail and it took about 3 weeks round trip to get answers to letters. Phone calls were an adventure and extremely expensive and so rarely happened.

Parent responses:

- Families need to make aliya together and go to a place with a strong American presence or they will fall through the cracks. Check your Zionism or ideology at the door because it will be used against you and you could make poor decisions. Figure out how to educate your kids K-12 because the education is deficient. Administrations care more about your political loyalty than your children's welfare, so tread carefully.

- It is not worth getting frustrated. Your child is an adult and is going to ultimately make their own decision.

- Do the army and learn the language.

- Start the conversation with your kids, learn to listen to what they are saying and trust them.
- Be better prepared, it might take longer to complete aliya but the process and everything that comes with it will move along more smoothly for everyone.
- Make sure you understand details.
- There's always a first one in each family. It was hard for her, hard for us in America. I used to say that I felt like someone had done open heart surgery without anesthesia. I worried about her and missed her, but knew 100% it was the right thing. Afterward, another child went, and then a third. When the fourth said she was going, we went too. Now we are ALL in Israel! What a blessing! So much better than having the family half in one place, half in another. I KNOW my grandchildren. I know my sons and daughters-in-law. Not just from a once-a-year visit. This is the ultimate blessing. And my first gets the credit for jumping in when it was tough! She became the home port, the anchor, for other siblings on a gap year, yeshiva, seminary and ultimately their and our aliya.
- As a parent of an oleh and lone soldier, I learned you need to push and be persistent about your and your family's needs. In Israel, they have only one volume—loud.
- If the child who wants to make aliya is truly committed, it is their choice. It is hard enough to be so far away, don't put any additional barriers in the relationship.
- Not easy but be supportive and always welcome to come back home.
- Try and support your child although it is hard.
- Be as prepared as possible. And make whatever sacrifices you need to say goodbye proudly and supportively.
- Remember the goals and aspirations.
- If you put it off, it doesn't happen.

- Love your kids and support their dreams. I speak to my children every single day, unless they didn't have their phones in the IDF. We are unbelievably close and they know I am here for anything and everything—the good, the bad, and the ugly.

- NBN is not the parent. They will treat your child like an adult, not like a teenager making aliya. You will not be in the loop because your child is older than 18. They mean well, but don't assume anything. Especially don't assume that they can ensure your child understands everything that is happening. Support your child in the process as best you can, and get as much information directly from NBN as you can and/or have your child show/forward you everything.

- Buckle up. It is going to be quite a ride.

- Seek out more support for religious girls serving in combat to keep them connected to learning.

- I have suggested to several parents that a gap year in Israel is a minimum, and it is a great experience. My son learned to be very independent.

- Parents and their oleh should keep a positive attitude and an open mind throughout the aliya process. It can be a very difficult decision and process on both sides, and each should hear the other's points of view. Always support your oleh and let them know you are there for them. The distance between you is not only going to be difficult for the parent to navigate but for the oleh as well, so the more support the oleh has, the better it can be for your relationship. Apps such as WhatsApp and FaceTime are a huge help to keep everyone in touch until you can visit.

- Try to have a good understanding why your child wants to make aliya. Listen to your child. Don't be in denial.

- Going through the army and college in Israel made for a smoother aliya.

- Be open to it.
- Keep your eyes wide open, continue gathering information, ask for support.
- Start early and do the process with your kids.
- The culture is more different than we assume. Learning the language is critical. Garin Tzabar is amazing in helping make this transition successful. Be supportive of your son or daughter if you want to help them be successful.
- In Israel, it is common for students to be older as many complete the army first and then travel. There is no pressure to go straight from high school to university.
- Support your child in their life decisions even though it might be hard on you.
- Moving away from family is very hard.
- Ask other parents for advice and details.
- Lots of savlanut (patience)!
- Trust your children. It isn't an easy journey for anyone especially if they join the IDF but our son has made a great success of his aliya and we are very proud of him—but miss him!
- Be open to it.
- Put serious effort into learning Hebrew well.
- Have more open discussions about the ability of the oleh to "fall" religiously and figure out ways to prevent that. We never had imagined that "falling" could be a byproduct of the aliya process.
- Your age at the time of aliya matters. Communication is key.
- Keep in touch, offer love and support to your child as they make these life-changing decisions.
- Our child did an excellent job of laying out his plans, so really the only thing would be a longer prep time so we'd be psychologically ready when it happened.

- Give your children the wings to fly and the confidence to make their own good decisions in life. Everyone is unique and has a different calling. Let them be who they are even if it's hard and you'll miss them. Of course, help them (in a healthy way) get settled and live there and as much as you can in every way. Appreciate the passion.

- The education system needs serious reform and needs small classrooms with care for children. They need to be nonpolitical so a kid doesn't have to be part of an ideology to feel accepted. There needs to be a no bullying policy in the schools...and in the country in general. The housing crisis needs a resolution because it's difficult to make aliya and rent for years with no stability or protection.

- My son actually met a girl while in yeshiva before making aliya (planned long before he met her) and they got married soon after aliya, so his experiences were not typical.

- For me, my relationship with my son was so important that during the month prior to my his aliya, we came up with rules for our relationship, like WhatsApp video once a week and always providing truthful answers to my questions.

- Parents and children should not be antagonists. They should realize they are on the same side and work together. Better understanding on the part of parents that just because a child chooses to take a different path in life, it doesn't mean they are against you and your life choices, or are questioning what/who you are. Children ought to also understand what a parent might be going through as they seek their independence.

- Make sure your oleh has an adopted family in Israel they can count on.

- Setting up banking was a time-consuming chore and many banks do not like working with new olim.

- Child's aliya has changed my thoughts about personal

aliya. Will likely be making aliya in the next few years and hoping other adult children will do so as well.

- I have an older son who made aliya several years prior to my daughter. Her process was the one in which I was most involved.

- I just wish there were no COVID-19 so I could see them and hug them. I miss them terribly.

- NBN should have an option to allow young olim to loop their parents in on the process even if the parents aren't making aliya. If the prospective oleh gives permission, there aren't privacy issues. Copy the parents on everything if the oleh allows. If not, they should be extra careful to be super clear and give extra attention and support.

- How am I? I am in awe of my daughter, a lone soldier. I am amazed by her courage and her commitment, and I am frustrated that I don't know how to help her. I am thankful to the families who adopted my daughter.

- She never considered what comes next after the army. I see this as typical for soldiers transitioning from the army. There is an abyss. Privately, I worry that she will be swallowed up by this dark hole.

- I think that my husband and I feel differently than other American parents because we made aliya and served ourselves.

- We are on the 36- to 38-year aliya plan and hope to move in the next couple of years. When we got married 36 years ago, we knew we always wanted to live in Israel but we haven't made it yet, hoping to get there in the next couple of years.

- I would recommend Garin Tzabar for making aliya with army service.

- Our daughter making aliya has led to our planning to make aliya as well.

- Dump your old mindset and expectations, strengthen your patience muscles and you'll be fine.
- It is painful to let your child go and not be able to see him/her when convenient. However, our child was very organized and respectful throughout the process.

Appendix B: Useful IDF Shorthand

שעת טש — שעת
טרום שינה

One hour of free time for soldiers to make their beds at night, get in line to shower, brush their teeth, and use whatever time is left for personal calls.

משקית תש — תנאי שירות

Note how similar it is to the term above. This is the word for the army personnel (usually a woman) who makes sure IDF soldiers have everything they need. This individual is supposed to ensure lone soldier rights and basic needs, from Hebrew to furniture. And this is the person lone soldiers must pester all the time.

אני סוגר

I am closing, which means they are on base for Shabbat or holidays.

תורנות

General army duties like kitchen duty, guarding, extra upkeep on the base, sweeping the leaves into the dust or the desert, taking out the trash.

טירונית

Note that this sounds similar to the one above. This one means basic training.

שעות ביציאה

Literally means hours for going out and it is a punishment, delaying a soldier's exit from base depending on the violation.

קו vs אימון   Once combat soldiers finish training, they switch every couple of months to protect an area known as a *kav*, a line. They can often return to *imun*, which includes additional training with other groups.

תג   Shoulder tag that identifies the base or unit you are part of.

סיכה   A pin that identifies the type of job you have.

כומתה   Beret, which they will promptly shave down so it isn't fuzzy. Everyone does it, and we really don't know why, but it clogs up our sink.

צ׳ופר   *Tshupar* is a present for doing something good.

Appendix C: Glossary of Terms

Acharei hachagim: "After the holidays," which more or less means anytime after Sukkot but before Passover, or any time immediately following any holiday, large or small. Sometimes used as an excuse to put things off.

Achuz neichut: Percentage of handicap—i.e., what percentage of the body isn't functioning.

Amalot: Fees and charges.

Arev: Guarantor.

Arnona: Local property taxes paid to the municipality. Olim receive a 90% discount on *arnona* their first year of aliya.

Asmachta: Receipt or document number.

Atzma'i: Independent contractor or freelancer with limited social benefits.

B'dika: Test.

B'dikat dam: Blood test.

Bagrut/Bagruyot: High school exams, generally in 11th and 12th grades. The exam period often starts after Passover and can continue through mid-July, in 11th and 12th grades.

Bayit rek: Empty house without parents, which immediately triggers a request for friends to hang out at the empty house.

Beinishim (Bnei yeshiva): Boys who are in yeshiva and draft for shortened active service of 16 to 18 months.

Beit mirkachat: Pharmacy.

Bituach briyut: Health insurance—in this case, reflected in your pay stub as a deduction to cover the socialized medical system.

Bituach chova: Compulsory car insurance.

Bituach Leumi: Behemoth government institution that manages the entire social welfare net for the country.

Bituach makif: Comprehensive car insurance (but really both types are needed).

Bituach rechev: Car insurance.

Bnot Sherut: National Service volunteers.

Bruto maskoret: Gross salary vs. "neto," your net.

Chagei Tishrei: All of the holidays that fall during the Jewish month of Tishrei—Rosh Hashana, Yom Kippur, and Sukkot. Not much school learning is done during this time period.

Chagim: Jewish holidays of all kinds.

Chagim leumi'im: National holidays within a one-week period and that fall right after Passover—Holocaust Remembrance Day, Memorial Day, and Independence Day.

Chayal boded: A lone soldier without parents in Israel.

Chofshi chodshi: Monthly bus pass reflected in your salary as part of the employer's coverage of your transportation costs.

Chok HaShvut: 1950s law called the Right of Return that grants every Jew, everywhere, the right to become an Israeli citizen.

Chozeh: Contract, employment and rentals.

Chug/Chugim: In academic setting, it means a course of study. In the context of young chidren, it is after-school activities.

Container: Your lift. There is no Hebrew word for lift and instead it is referred to as a "container" in Hebrew.

D'mei havra'a: Convalescence pay, which is designed to help employees take vacation and is generally paid in the summer months.

Dachash (D'chiyat sherut): Deferral of service.

Delek: Gasoline.

Dood shemesh/Dood: Solar heating system for water on the roof of a building.

Erev chag: Day before any holiday, when there is normally no school.

Ezrach chozer: An Israeli citizen born abroad to at least one parent who held Israeli citizenship at the time of birth.

Frier: Fool.

Garin Tzabar: Group of IDF recruits who make aliya together, live together, and go through the IDF evaluation process together.

Ha'avara bankait: Wire transfer.

Hafkada: Deposit.

Hafkadat check patuach: Open check that is signed—in this context, for utilities.

Hafnaya: Referral.

Halacha: Jewish law.

Halachic: Applying Jewish religious standards.

Hamra'a matach: Exchange of foreign currency (matach stands for matbe'a chutz, foreign currency).

Haramat kosit: A toast, usually a gathering before Rosh Hashana or Passover.

Hardal: Haredi Leumi, those who are more aligned with ultra-Orthodox lifestyles but who are more Zionistic and nationalistic.

Haredi: "Trembling" before God, referring to the ultra-Orthodox population, some of whom do not consider themselves Zionist.

Hesder: IDF-approved program that offers two years of yeshiva learning followed by a maximum of 18 months of IDF active service and ending with another two years of yeshiva learning.

Hitchayvut: Commitment by the kupa to pay for an appointment or a procedure.

Hora'at keva: Standing order to withdraw money from your account to pay a supplier or a company on a monthly basis.

Ishur: Approval.

Jewish Agency: Known in Hebrew as the Sochnut Ha'Yehudit. In addition to Misrad HaKlita, olim will also face Misrad Hapnim, the Ministry of the Interior, quite early in their aliya.

Kaban (katzin l'briyut nefesh): Mental health officer.

Kartis ashra'i: Credit card.

Kaspomat: ATM.

Katin chozer: Someone who received Israeli citizenship in Israel and left before the age of 14.

Keren hishtalmut: Optional benefit in which employee contributes 2.5% of salary and employer contributes 5 or 7.5%.

Kfiya datit: Religious coercion in the school system.

Klita: Absorption into Israeli society.

Kupa: Health insurance plan.

Kupat holim: The socialized medicine single payer system. You ought to choose the strongest in your area and you can switch plans every quarter.

Laila lavan: White nights, pretty much staying up all night.

Lift: Israelis call a lift a "container," and it sounds like "con-tay-ner."

Lishkat HaGiyus: IDF recruitment office. No one is allowed in there other than recruits or soldiers—no parents, siblings, or friends allowed.

M'fakdim: Commanding officers.

M'gamot: Electives that you take starting in 10th grade.

M'shicha: Withdrawal from an account.

M'zuman: Cash.

Ma'am (mas erech musaf): VAT.

Ma ha'kesher: Figuratively, "What's your point?" Literally, "How is that connected?"

Mahal: Division of the IDF that allows for noncitizens to volunteer in the IDF for 18 months rather than full required service.

Makolet: Small neighborhood hole-in-the-wall supermarket.

Mamlachti Dati: State religious school.

Mamlachti: State secular school.

Mangal: Barbecue—it's both a noun and a verb.

Mas Hachnasa: Israel's Income Tax Authority.

Masa kumta: Long journey carrying quite a bit of heavy gear to receive your beret.

Mashakit Tash: Army office responsible for the conditions of your service.

Matnas: Mercaz l'tarbut, nofesh v'sport, a local community center (every community has one) for culture, leisure, and sports.

Me'onot: Day care centers.

Meches: Israeli tax authority that operates at the ports of entry to evaluate the costs of items shipped to Israel. Meches decides whether to let the package through and decides whether tax should be added to the purchase.

Mechina/Mechina K'dam Tzva'it: Pre-army academies, a 12- to 18-month program prior to the army that is very Israeli in nature and is approved by the Ministry of Defense.

Mechina: As applied to university, it is a prepratory program before your actual studies begin.

Michveh Alon: A special army base for soldiers who made

aliya with insufficient Hebrew. The purpose is to give them intensive language and cultural courses to help them adjust.

Midrasha: 12- to 24-month gap year program, approved by the Ministry of Defense, that focuses heavily on Jewish texts of all kinds.

Minus: Pronounced "mee-noose," and it means that you have a negative balance in your bank account.

Mirpeset: Porch.

Mirsham: Prescription.

Mishpacha m'ametzet: Adopted family.

Mispar bank: Bank number. All banks have numbers, then branch numbers, then your bank account number.

Mispar heshbon: Bank account number.

Misrad HaBitachon: Ministry of Defense.

Misrad HaBriyut: Ministry of Health.

Misrad HaKlita: Ministry of Absorption and Immigration. One of the first stops an oleh makes. The Ministry arranges for the "sal klita" to be transferred, government money to help you get on your feet, which an oleh receives for six months. It also pays for *ulpan*, Hebrew immersion class, directly.

Misrah: Job position or posting.

Mivchan Yael: Timed Hebrew proficiency exam.

Miyunim: Filtering or sorting process via testing by the IDF to place a recruit in an army position.

Mo'ed bet: "Do-over" test in case you don't do well enough on the first exam.

Moomcheh: Specialist.

Morah or **rakaz l'olim:** Teacher/coordinator in school who is required to assist new immigrants.

Nahag chadash: New driver up to the age of 24, for whom car insurance is quite expensive.

Nekudot zikui: Tax credits that apply to olim, single parents, those who served in the IDF/ National Service, and others.

Olah vatika/oleh vatik: Oleh who has been in Israel a long time.

Osek mursheh: Small business that otherwise operates as a regular business above a certain income amount.

Osek patur: Small business for which value-added tax is waived under a certain income amount.

P'tor: Waiver from IDF service.

Pazam (Perek z'mani minimali): Minimal amount of time left for service in the IDF.

Pensia, kupot gemel, and bituach minhalim: Terms related to private pension fund deductions that are required by law.

Pikadon: Deposit—in this case, some kind of security deposit to protect property.

Pinkas shek: Checkbook.

Pitzuim: Severance pay.

Protekzia: Connections.

Rabbanut: Rabbinate of the State of Israel.

Ram shtayim (r'shima m'kuvetzet): A grouped list that really doesn't explain why this unit has this name. It is colloquially known as Ram shtayim, a status an injured soldier is in when he or she cannot serve in their unit.

Ribit: Interest.

Rishayon rechev: Annual cost for your license plate. Similar to car registration.

Rofeh mishpacha: Family doctor or primary care physician.

Sachir: Salaried employee.

Sal klita: Absorption basket, a fixed sum of money paid by the government for a six-month period.

Sapak: A supplier or service provider.

Sh'vuz (Shover et hazayin): Literally breaking one down.

Shalat (Sherut l'lo tashlum): Service without payment, equivalent to administrative unpaid leave.

Shalom kita aleph: Ceremonies held around the country on the Shabbat before children start first grade. It's more important than their college graduation.

Sherut Leumi: National Service for those who have an IDF waiver.

Shivyon ba'netel: Equalization of societal burdens.

Shnat sherut: Year of volunteer service in a program approved by the Ministry of Defense.

Sika: A pin that identifies the type of job you have.

Sikum: Summary of a meeting or an appointment

Snif (prounounced "sneef"): Bank branch number, generally your local bank.

T'lush maskoret: Israeli pay stub. The law requires every employee to receive it monthly.

Tafsiki lachfor: Stop digging or needling me.

Tag: Shoulder tag that identifies your base or unit.

Tashlumim: Payment plan to spread out payments for a given purchase, normally without "ribit," interest.

Tashtit: Infrastructure—of any kind. It can mean internet infrastructure or road infrastructure.

Te'um mas: Coordination of income so that you don't pay double tax when you hold more than one job.

Tekes hash'ba'a: Swearing in ceremony.

Terem: Stands for tipul refui miyadi, which is a free standing urgent center, usually open 24 hours.

Teudat oleh: Looks similar to a passport, reflects your aliya date, and is often used by tax authorities to stamp information on your rights. You will need it when you go to the tax authorities for your lift, for example, or when you buy a car. Don't throw away your teudat oleh even after you are no longer an oleh.

Teudat zehut: Blue identity card that you are required by law to carry with you at all times.

Teum mas: Coordination of income tax to ensure that you don't pay double taxes when working at two separate employers.

Tik: File that you open in any government office.

Tilboshet achida: School uniform.

Tnuat no'ar: Youth groups.

Tofes 101 (kartis oved): Worker's card that is more like a form every employee completes every year.

Toshav chozer: Citizens of Israel who were 17 or older at the time of returning to Israel, who were considered an Israeli resident in the past, and who resided outside of Israel at least two years. There are other complicated criteria related to this status.

Tz'yun magen: Overall score for the year, before the *bagrut* exam score.

Tzav rishon: Initial IDF draft orders received by a recruit.

Tzaharon: After-school activities for younger children, sometimes within the school building itself.

Tzimirim: Quaint cabins throughout the country.

Ulpan: Hebrew language immersion class, with tests to evaluate levels and progress.

Va'ad bayit: Residents' committee and the monthly fees that go toward communal upkeep of the common areas of the building.

Y'chidot: Number of points for each high school course, ranging from three to five points.

Yemei keif: Fun days (for employees, teams or friends).

Yerida: Leaving Israel.

Yeutz: Advice or consultancy. In the context of health care, it means to see a specialist.

Yom Ha'Atzmaut: Israel's Independence Day, celebrated right after sunset on Memorial Day.

Yom HaZikaron: Israel's Memorial Day remembering those who died in service of the country or in terror attacks.

Yom siddurim: Extra days off for lone soldiers to run errands.

Yunkers: Gas heating system.

Endnotes

Introduction

1 Central Bureau of Statistics, accessed https://www.cbs.gov.il/he/mediarelease/DocLib/2020/223/21_20_223e.pdf.

2 The Central Bureau of Statistics data in 2019 grouped olim between 15-64 in one band. To determine the data on ages 15-34, we calculated the age band data from this chart: https://www.cbs.gov.il/he/mediarelease/doclib/2020/223/21_20_223t6.pdf.

3 Maltz, J., Haaretz, October 29, 2019. Hebrew: https://www.haaretz.co.il/100/judaism/.premium-MAGAZINE-1.8054107.

4 Maltz, J., Haaretz, July 28, 2020. "Israel's leading demographer warns of post-COVID-19 exodus by young, educated Israelis." https://www.haaretz.com/israel-news/.premium-demographer-warns-of-post-pandemic-covid-19-coronavirus-exodus-israelis-1.9024614?fbclid=IwAR1B_v8wyEbkYqyRwQ4dNBHEQ_HcmPfq66A9vsgPAGuflS5FIPXnwsTiJBU.

Chapter 1

1 Accessed on August 6, 2020: https://www.cnbc.com/2017/10/13/money-advice-from-benjamin-franklins-book-on-wealth.html.

2 Supra footnote 2.

3 Central Bureau of Statistics, accessed https://www.cbs.gov.il/he/mediarelease/DocLib/2020/223/21_20_223e.pdf.

4 The Central Bureau of Statistics data in 2019 grouped olim between 15-64 in one band. To determine the data on ages 15-34, we calculated the age band data from this chart: https://www.cbs.gov.il/he/mediarelease/doclib/2020/223/21_20_223t6.pdf.

5 This chapter and this book do not address gap-year programs that are rooted in the ultra-Orthodox sector, where young men come to Israel to learn in those frameworks and may or may not make aliya. More often than not, these young men do not consider college, either in Israel or outside of it, as an option for them. Hence, this chapter's discussion on college does not apply to this group.

6 From Joe O'Shea's book, Gap Year: How Delaying College Changes People in Ways the World Needs.

7 We have not been able to locate peer-reviewed research on the impact

of Israeli gap-year programs and therefore assume that the generalities noted above more or less apply conceptually.

8   Universities are academic institutions of higher learning that have Ph.D. tracks. All others are colleges that offer degrees up and through masters' level. The Council for Higher Education in Israel has regulatory authority over both universities and colleges.

9   Unable to travel to his medical practice in America due to the COVID-19 pandemic, Dr. Jason Cohen and his family created Holy Butter peanut butter.

Chapter 2

1   Accessed on August 6, 2020: https://www.youtube.com/watch?v=Iyv905Q2omU.

2   https://www.timesofisrael.com/past-decade-saw-over-a-quarter-million-immigrants-to-israel-from-150-countries/ December 21, 2019.

3   For instance, 2018 saw 2740 North American olim and 2017 saw 2847. https://www.cbs.gov.il/he/mediarelease/doclib/2019/206/21_19_206t2.pdf.

Chapter 3

1   Carroll, Lewis, Alice's Adventures in Wonderland, Chapter 6. Accessed on August 6, 2020 at: https://www.forbes.com/sites/greggfairbrothers/2011/11/29/going-somewhere-2/#284a316d431e.

Chapter 4

1   Disney movie, Aladdin, as said by Genie. Accessed August 6, 2020 at: https://screenrant.com/disney-aladdin-best-quotes/

2   See Nefesh B'Nefesh's site for more information on costs of shipping and consult with others on the types of items that might be worth shipping.

3   Those who make aliya from Israel, on some level, deprive themselves of the closure that happens at the airport.

Chapter 5

1   Erika Anderson, Forbes 2013. Accessed on August 6, 2020 at https://

www.forbes.com/sites/erikaandersen/2013/01/10/10-quotes-from-the-first-lady-of-the-world/#64531a3e272b

2   https://www.cbs.gov.il/he/mediarelease/
DocLib/2019/378/15_19_378b.pdf

Chapter 6

1   Accessed on August 6, 2020 at: https://www.youtube.com/watch?v=q-9kPks0IfE

Chapter 7

1   Winston Churchill. (n.d.). AZQuotes.com. Retrieved September 20, 2020, from AZQuotes.com website: https://www.azquotes.com/quote/56404.

2   The moral cognitive dissonance that soldiers face is a real one, particularly those in combat duty. Those who attend pre-army Mechinot are a bit more prepared for these difficult and often painful judgment calls than those who arrive in Israel thinking that there is some sort of clear defining line.

3   Literally translated as breaking one's male member.

4   See, for instance, the post from Razyl Cylich on what to expect when drafting as a lone soldier. https://www.facebook.com/rayzl.cylich?__tn__=%2CdCH-R-R&eid=ARBWbONiPMB9ktjvXY_P8EMPbU-0ipgK7bykoc EiDf5qmfuAF10S5zDJnx4P61gtUZymSAqsVq2ZXJuG&hc_ref=ARR8n0Sn6pybzBckvRf1sJX5Hgt0I2Keip1Ert3jqrOnuTQyzySD uUGhH2WoxFmRBGY&fref=nf.

5   During the period we wrote this book, the mandatory service years changed from 2.7 years to 2.5 years, a good example of how often the "rules" change.

6   Criteria for psychological or physical waivers are not addressed here.

7   See Haaretz's 2019 report "What Is Killing Israel's Lone Soldiers," https://www.haaretz.com/israel-news/MAGAZINE-israel-army-idf-lone-soldiers-suicide-military-1.7729693.

8   See https://www.mevaker.gov.il/sites/DigitalLibrary/Documents/2018-68b-104-bodedim.pdf; https://www.ynetnews.com/articles/0,7340,L-5447983,00.html (Jan 18, 2019). The Lone Soldier Center reports it at 7,000, of which 45% are immigrants (around 3,150).

9   Sometime during the first two years of *Hesder*, the IDF continues its "sorting" process to determine where the recruit should be assigned when the time comes.

10   In cases where an oleh received an e-mail from Nefesh B'Nefesh indicating the he or she is exempt, this exemption shall suffice.

11   Gal, R.; Amit, K.; Fleisher, N.; Strichman, N., 2003. Volunteers of National Youth Service in Israel: A Study on Motivation for Service, Social Attitudes and Volunteers' Satisfaction. Center for Social Development.

12   Sherer, M., 2004. National Service in Israel: Motivations, Volunteer Characteristics, and Levels of Content, Nonprofit and Voluntary Sector Quarterly, vol. 33, no. 1.

13   Footnote 12, supra.

Chapter 8

1   Jon Stewart Commencement Speech, 2004, College of William and Mary. Accessed on August 6, 2020 at: https://www.wm.edu/news/stories/2004/jon-stewarts-84-commencement-address.php.

2   Any institution of higher education in Israel is called "university" if it is able to grant Ph.D.s. Any institution that does not have the authority to grant a doctorate will be called a "college."

3   Haaretz, October 2015. https://www.haaretz.com/israel-news/.premium-no-frat-parties-israel-has-oldest-students-in-the-world-1.5414408.

4   OECD Country Report 2019, https://www.oecd.org/education/education-at-a-glance/EAG2019_CN_ISR.pdf.

5   https://www.idc.ac.il/en/pages/home.aspx.

6   https://overseas.huji.ac.il.

7   https://biuinternational.com.

8   Israeli university tuition is around 15,000 NIS per year. Private universities with English programs can be 60,000 NIS.

9   Master's degrees might pose a different set of challenges but probably not as great as the linguistic and cultural ones facing bachelor's degree students who enroll at younger ages.

Chapter 9

1 Approval for use of quote received via e-mail on June 16, 2020.

2 https://www.gov.il/en/Departments/General/introducing_innovative_reforms.

3 See https://www.calcalistech.com/ctech/articles/0,7340,L-3769660,00.html, accessed August 27, 2020.

4 http://taubcenter.org.il/wp-content/files_mf/womenandparents_eng.pdf.

5 In September 2019, for example, there were a total of nine business days.

6 Perhaps with the exception of Hanukah.

7 See Yehudit Abrams Facebook post, August 31, 2020, https://www.facebook.com/diana.prince.9237/posts/10164155967000302.

8 The average home price is nearly eight times the average household income, a declining share of young families own their homes, and there are a myriad of complex policy decisions that have caused the housing crisis. See OECD Economic Surveys, Israel 2018: http://www.oecd.org/economy/surveys/Israel-2018-OECD-economic-survey-overview.pdf.

Chapter 10

1 Dr. Seuss, Oh the Places You'll Go, accessed text August 18, 2020, at https://genius.com/Dr-seuss-oh-the-places-youll-go-excerpt-annotated.

Chapter 11

1 https://www.timesofisrael.com/rabbis-making-it-harder-for-immigrants-to-prove-jewishness-advocate-says/. Also see the organization ITIM a non-profit committed to increasing participation in Jewish life by making Israel's religious establishment respectful of and responsive to the diverse Jewish needs of the Jewish people. https://www.itim.org.il/en/.

Chapter 12

1 See https://dictionary.cambridge.org/dictionary/english/financial-literacy, accessed August 21, 2020.

2   See https://www.nbn.org.il/aliyahpedia/getting-started-planning-aliyah/financial-planning/budgeting-first-year-aliyah/.

3   See https://www.calcalistech.com/ctech/articles/0,7340,L-3769660,00.html, accessed August 27, 2020.

4   See https://www.calcalistech.com/ctech/articles/0,7340,L-3769660,00.html, accessed August 27, 2020.

5   See fn. 3 and 4 supra.

6   See fn. 3 and 4 supra.

7   https://www.cbs.gov.il/he/mediarelease/DocLib/2019/378/15_19_378b.pdf.

8   See https://www.nbn.org.il/aliyahpedia/government-services/drivers-license-cars/converting-foreign-drivers-license/.

9   https://www.maariv.co.il/news/military/Article-761687. Hebrew.

10 https://www.calcalist.co.il/local/articles/0,7340,L-3724838,00.html. Hebrew.

Chapter 13

1   Sarah Dessen, Keeping the Moon, accessed https://www.goodreads.com/work/quotes/100634-keeping-the-moon. Book website accessed https://sarahdessen.com/book/keeping-the-moon/.

2   Gilbert, Martin, "In Ishmael's House: A History of Jews in Arab Lands," 2010, Yale University Press, an historical review of the life of Jews in Arab lands.

3   2020 Central Bureau of Statistics, accessed https://www.cbs.gov.il/he/mediarelease/Pages/2020/-בחול-ששהו-ישראלים-של-2018--בשנת-וחזרות-יציאות שנה-ויותר-ברציפות.aspx. It is important to note that the statistics noted in this chapter focus on the number of Israelis leaving the country. It does not reflect the net differential between Israelis who leave and Israelis who return, but which is reported by CBS.

4   Dan Ben-David, "Leaving the Promised Land, A Look at Israel's Emigration Challenge," Shoresh Institute for Socioeconomic Research, Department of Public Policy, Tel Aviv University, 2019.

5   See "Leaving the Promised Land," Shoresh Institute.

6   Supra, fn 5.

7   Supra, fn 5.

8   See footnote 3 supra.

9   Joseph Chamie, Barry Mirkin, "The Million Missing Israelis," Foreign Policy, July 5, 2011. https://foreignpolicy.com/2011/07/05/the-million-missing-israelis/

10   (https://www.jpost.com/jerusalem-report/what-happened-to-aliyah-from-france-581237; https://www.israelhayom.com/2019/07/10/without-an-emergency-plan-french-jews-will-stop-making-aliyah/).

11   Press reports include: "You've Made Aliya, Now What?" Tablet Magazine, October 2017 (https://www.tabletmag.com/sections/news/articles/youve-made-aliyah-now-what). "Why My Friends Are Leaving Israel (Russian perspective), Ynet, January 2013, https://www.ynetnews.com/articles/1,7340,L-4334357,00.html). "Olim Who Came Back to U.S. Describe the Challenges of Aliya," Jewish Chronicle, May 2017, (https://jewishchronicle.timesofisrael.com/olim-who-came-back-to-u-s-describe-challenges-of-aliyah/). "The Difficulties and Regrets of Recent Olim," The Jerusalem Post, March 2018, https://www.pressreader.com/israel/jerusalem-post-magazine/20180302/282248076058477.

Other sources include comments from Facebook posts, Secret Jerusalem, June 18, 2020, Sammy Katz.

12   https://www.maariv.co.il/news/military/Article-761687. Hebrew.

13   https://www.calcalist.co.il/local/articles/0,7340,L-3724838,00.html. Hebrew.

14   See footnote 11 supra.

15   https://fs.knesset.gov.il/20/law/20_lsr_343926.pdf.

16   A debt of gratitude goes to our friends Drs. Dassi and Dan Jacobson, whose wise words have been a staple of our existence for all these years.

17   Theodore Herzl, Altneuland (Old-New Land), 1902. See Epilogue section. https://www.wzo.org.il/index.php?dir=site&page=articles&op=item&cs=3494&langpage=eng.

Conclusions

1   From the song, "I Have No Other Country," written by Ehud Manor in memory of his brother and performed by Gal Atari. https://www.youtube.com/watch?v=MEJ5jgCaDhE.

2   March 1969-September 1970.

About the Authors

Ariella Bernstein was born in Philadelphia, Pennsylvania, and raised in Lawrence, New York. She spent nearly 20 years in Federal sector labor law in the United States and since making aliya in 2009 has held a variety of positions in the nonprofit sector. She works in investor relations and volunteers in Jerusalem's tech sector ecosystem as a mentor to start-ups.

Photo by Yael Ilan

Avi Losice was born in Albany, New York. He spent 25 years in the financial sector, working for Standard and Poor's, and more than five years at the Securities and Exchange Commission, a position that kept him in the United States when the family made aliya. Since making aliya in 2015, he has been a consultant for the Israel Securities Authority.

This book was borne out of their experiences as olim and their encounters with other olim but, most importantly, the range of emotions we *all* experienced during our aliya journey. They wrote this book as a letter home to prospective olim and their families, hoping that others can learn from their experiences.

The authors are always open to questions and can be reached at **aliyajourneyhome@gmail.com**.

For bulk orders of this book, please visit our website, **www.aliyajourney.com**

Coming Soon!

ALIYA: Unsung Heroes

There are heroes among the tens of thousands of olim who immigrate to Israel every year—olim who left their place of birth, overcame challenges, and made a difference in Israeli society—yet you probably never heard their names. These are their stories.

ALIYA: Retiring Home

They deferred their dreams, working for decades preparing for the day when they could retire "home." Retiring in Israel comes with its own unique social, familial, and economic challenges retirees should keep in mind before they live the dream in their golden years.

www.aliyajourney.com

Made in the USA
Middletown, DE
19 March 2021

35909612R00168